ONE LORD
ONE FAITH

Ecumenical Services for the Christian Year

STUART THOMAS

Kevin Mayhew

First published in 2000 by
KEVIN MAYHEW LTD
Buxhall, Stowmarket
Suffolk IP14 3BW

The publishers wish to express their gratitude to
NewStart 2000 Ltd for permission to include the
Prayer of Renewal which is taken from Worship Resources
for the Millennium, Volume 2, copyright NewStart 2000 Ltd.

0 1 2 3 4 5 6 7 8 9

ISBN 1 84003 570 6
Catalogue Number 1500361

Cover design by Jonathan Stroulger
Edited by Helen Elliot
Typesetting by Richard Weaver
Printed and bound in Great Britain

For Heather
without whose patience and encouragement
this book would never have happened

FOREWORD

I am delighted to commend this book of ecumenical services and am personally grateful to Stuart Thomas for producing it.

Nowhere is our unity in Jesus Christ made more visible than in shared worship. There is nothing like the opportunity of prayer and reflection together to remind us all of how much, in Christ, we need each other. I hope that this book will increase our confidence in seeking and using every opportunity to be together on the journey of faith and in the worship of God.

Rt Revd John Gladwin
Bishop of Guildford

CONTENTS

Introduction 7

SETTING THE ECUMENICAL SCENE

Change and decay in all around I see . . . 11

Three good reasons why 12

Overcoming the obstacles 14

57 varieties? 15

Setting off on the right track . . . 16

Getting the show on the road . . . 17

External influences 18

Service options 19

Resources 21

How to use this book/these services 21

THE CHRISTIAN YEAR

Overview 25

Advent Sunday 26

Advent service 27

A reflective service for Advent 29

The Christmas service 32

Epiphany 35

A penitential service for the beginning of Lent 38

A reflective service for Lent 44

Mothering Sunday or A celebration of the family 46

Palm Sunday 49

Good Friday 51

Easter, Ascension and Pentecost 58

Easter evening praise 59

Ascensiontide 61

Pentecost 63

Harvest Festival 65

All Saints' Day 68

OTHER OCCASIONS

Week of Prayer for Christian Unity   75

Christian Aid Week   78

Remembrance   81

Evangelistic services   83

Healing services   86

Civic services   90

A New Year/New Start service   93

INTRODUCTION

'Isn't this a bit worrying?' asked Maggie, my churchwarden at the time, as she pointed to an ominous-looking crack which had appeared on a pillar by my vestry, and tested it with her finger. Her colleague, Margaret, came over to survey the damage. 'Perhaps we ought to get the structural engineer back in,' she suggested, 'if only to make sure it's not a problem.' Not being a civil engineer I hadn't a clue how to react, but when I tried the crack for myself, my finger emerged with a coating of brick-dust and plaster. 'You remember what it was like last time,' I replied, 'but it looks like it needs checking out to me.'

Some four years previously our parish, far from the wealthiest in the area, had raised £60,000 to underpin part of the building, which had been suffering from severe cracking. It appeared to have been a success, and now we'd raised enough for a substantial interior refurbishment, but these new cracks looked alarming. At only 60 years old, no one would have expected St Francis of Assisi, Ewell, to be a strong candidate to become the first parish church building in Guildford Diocese to be demolished, but within two years of that first conversation its inadequate construction meant that we had to abandon the building for safety reasons. Two and a half years after that it was demolished.

It wasn't at all what I'd anticipated when I arrived in Ewell in 1994, full of hope and ideas. But among the many things this experience has taught me, two stand out:

1. It's easy to get carried away or overwhelmed by building and maintenance issues and forget our primary calling in Christ, to share his good news and love with others.

2. It's easy to forget that we don't stand alone in the Christian faith.

Of course I'd taken part in ecumenical activity before, as a curate in a town centre parish and then in my first incumbency. It was always good to meet with ministers of other traditions in the clergy fraternal, and in both those situations there had been good co-operation for one-off events. But the closure of our church building confronted me with a quite new situation, because, thanks to the generosity of our local Methodist church, we transferred our worship two hundred yards down the road to their building. Three years into this sharing agreement as I write, we now worship as a united congregation at major festivals, on other important occasions, and every Sunday evening. It has been a steep learning curve for all of us, and we certainly haven't reached the end of it yet, though both congregations have decided with much enthusiasm to fully unite all our worship.

I'm very glad that I now work in a situation where I have to co-operate with Christians from another tradition, though not proud that circumstances beyond my control pushed me into it. It hasn't always been the easiest of roads to travel, and occasionally we've been surprised at the seemingly trivial issues which have created a hiatus. At the same time, our shared worship has been uplifting and inspiring, making us realise that when we overcome the barriers of entrenched attitudes and resistance to change we can grow in our common faith far more than we thought possible.

This book contains resource material and outline services for a variety of ecumenical situations. Some of it has been 'road-tested' by our own congregation, some has been tried out elsewhere. It is offered in the hope and prayer that it will encourage more Christians to gather together for worship in their community across traditional boundaries. There has been considerable progress over the last three decades, but the Church's witness and impact is nonetheless still significantly weakened by division, disunity, and most often its refusal to move from its present position. Only as we overcome these barriers will we be brought nearer to the complete unity our Lord prayed for.

SETTING THE ECUMENICAL SCENE

CHANGE AND DECAY IN ALL AROUND I SEE . . .

The Bishop was visiting one of his more traditional parishes one Sunday morning, and before the service was greeted by an elderly and dour-looking churchwarden. Trying to make pleasant conversation and establish a rapport, the Bishop asked him sociably how long he had served in that capacity. 'Forty-five years,' came back the rather curt reply. The Bishop looked suitably amazed and impressed at this revelation. 'My goodness,' he said, 'that must be some kind of a record. I guess you've seen a lot of changes in that time.' The churchwarden replied grimly, 'You're right there, Bishop, I have – and I've opposed every single one of them!'

That story may have been embroidered in the telling, but it contains more than a grain of truth. We live in a world where everything changes so rapidly that the prospect of more change in almost any sphere makes us want to hang on even more tightly to the things we're familiar with, or which make us feel secure. This is especially true of the Church, which for many people provides the sense of comfort and timelessness they feel they need to cushion them against the uncertainties and pressures of modern life. Newspapers often carry reports of clergy who've fallen out with their congregations through trying to develop the style of music, make buildings more user-friendly, or abandon an outdated activity. And few changes arouse more fierce antipathy than 'tampering with the liturgy', a problem by no means restricted to the Church of England and the *Book of Common Prayer!*

At the same time, the pace of social change has forced Churches of all traditions to face the realities of modern life. No longer do they play such a key role in the community or carry so much weight of authority; no longer is their continued presence guaranteed; no longer do the majority of people see them as having much relevance to their everyday lives. Church attendance has declined seriously over the last three decades, particularly among the young, not least because there are so many competing activities on a Sunday. And while the financial situation may not be quite so black as some would like to paint it, neither is it exactly rose-coloured. Against this kind of backdrop it is not surprising that much has changed, despite frequent opposition.

Sociologists may have a field day analysing all these social trends and changes, as they try to explain what's happening, but that is not the purpose here. However, two interconnected factors within the Churches have had a major impact on the direction of change – the Charismatic Renewal and the Ecumenical Movement. The beginnings of modern Charismatic Renewal are usually traced to Los Angeles in 1906, though teaching on personal experience of the work of the Holy Spirit can certainly be traced back as far as the Wesleys and Methodism. Charismatic Renewal probably warrants a book in its own right, but so many have been written already that there is neither space nor need to add more here. Enough to say that, because of its influence on all denominations, many traditional barriers have been lowered if not broken down, and there has been a corresponding increase in awareness and acceptance of other Christian traditions.

The Ecumenical Movement (from the Greek word *oikoumenikos* meaning 'of the inhabited world') is usually reckoned to have its origins in Edinburgh in 1910, when the first International Missionary Conference was held, with over 1,000 delegates from around the world meeting across denominational divides. This led directly to the formation of the International Missionary Council in 1921, and indirectly (via the 'Faith and Order' and 'Life and Order' movements) of the World Council of Churches in 1948. These two bodies merged in 1961. The Roman Catholic Church is not a full member of the WCC, but it plays an increasing part. In the UK, the first local Councils of Churches were established as long ago as 1917 (in Bolton and Manchester), the British Council of Churches in 1942. Interestingly, while proposed schemes for uniting churches nationally came to nothing, it was local 'experiments' that started to flourish, leading to the term 'Local Ecumenical Project' being coined in 1973 (changed in 1995 to 'Partnership', and hereafter known for convenience as an LEP!). To provide

an umbrella organisation for all this varied ecumenical activity a new set of structures was
introduced in 1990: the Council of Churches
in Britain and Ireland (CCBI) is the co-ordinating body, made up of Churches Together in
England (CTE), Churches Together in Wales
(CYTUN) and Action of Churches Together in
Scotland (ACTS), with local expressions of
these in most communities throughout the
country. In addition there are now well over 400
LEPs operating from Cornwall to Caithness,
involving most mainstream denominations. No
one is going to pretend this has all been
straightforward, nor that it hasn't encountered
hostility en route. Perhaps the most significant
point is that progress has been made *despite*
animosity and apathy – in fact, LEPs have
flourished to a far greater extent in the UK than
almost anywhere else in the world, on a scale
approached only in Canada and New Zealand.

Many towns and districts now enjoy ecumenical worship from time to time, usually
organised by the local 'Churches Together'
group, but despite all that has happened, most
have found it quite hard to generate initial
support for this kind of initiative. There are
several reasons why:

1. Most churches are kept at full stretch trying
to survive, let alone aiming for growth, and
an additional service can become one burden
too many. If the regular Sunday evening
service is abandoned in favour of one taking
place elsewhere, it may be seen by some
regular worshippers as an excuse for an
'evening off'.

2. Within most congregations there is a range
of false assumptions about other Christian
denominations and traditions. Most of these
are untested, and many frankly unjustified.
Sadly, there is sometimes a marked reluctance even to check them out, let alone
revise them in the light of reality.

3. We find it difficult to accept that another
group of Christians may have a different but
equally valid approach to worship. We
become familiar and comfortable with one
approach, and feel uneasy when confronted
by an alternative liturgical style or musical
tradition. As a result we emphasise the dif-

ferences (usually fairly minor) rather than
our common faith in one Lord.

4. Ecumenical worship easily degenerates into
blandness. In a commendable effort to make
everyone feel included there is a real danger
of descending to the 'lowest common
denominator'. This may well avert critical
comments, but is unlikely to make much of
an impact on anyone, and leads in the end to
united services being seen as dull, stifling,
and best avoided if at all possible.

So much for the bad news. The good news is
that in some places this phase has been worked
through. There is now increasing willingness
to go beyond the occasional experiment in
worship across traditional boundaries. Instead,
effort is being made to bring the different
denominations together in a closer and more
lasting partnership. In some places this has
developed into a full-blown Local Ecumenical
Partnership being established, in which all the
participating churches sign a covenant formally
committing them to 'serve God together in their
local situation'.

THREE GOOD REASONS WHY

So what's the point of ecumenism? If people
have chosen the churches they want to attend,
why force something different on them? Isn't it
more important to get on with serving Christ,
spreading the Good News and making disciples than spending time on more meetings
and talking, and persuading people to accept
changes they don't want? If ecumenical
activity were the sole preserve of senior church
leaders these questions might well be asked
more frequently. But as we have seen, ecumenism has been most effective at the local
rather than the national level – the initiative
has come, by and large, from ordinary folk in
the pews.

There are three primary reasons for pursuing Christian Unity and nurturing it across
denominational boundaries:

1. Theological

Denominations are a relatively recent phenomenon in the history of the Church. Most of those we now accept as mainstream came into being in the wake of the Reformation. That is not to say that Christians in the Early Church didn't disagree and split up into factions – Paul clearly condemns just such a situation at Corinth (1 Corinthians 1:10-13) – but far from being regarded as the norm it was considered shameful, and a denial of all that the Christian faith stood for. And in an age when Christians were very likely to experience opposition and persecution for their faith, the last thing the Church needed was to be weakened by divisions.

In John 17, Jesus' profound 'High-priestly Prayer' makes it quite clear that one important outcome of his impending death was to bring unity among his followers (verse 23), an aspect of his teaching which his disciples and the early Christians took with the utmost seriousness. Christians did not need to pursue unity, because it was theirs already in Christ. Whatever minor personal disagreements they may have had, their unity was a public statement that they stood together in one faith under one Lord. To be disunited was to negate the very centre and raison d'être of their faith, the crucifixion and resurrection of Jesus Christ, and what this had achieved.

It was also an important part of Christian witness in the Early Church to be seen standing as one. As Jesus said, 'By this everyone will know that you are my disciples, if you have love one for another' (John 13:35). In the eyes of those outside the Church, then as now, the sight of Christians claiming to be followers of Jesus Christ yet arguing, disputing bitterly and splitting up into smaller groups which refuse to listen to or speak with each other was a cause of disenchantment and scorn. Sadly, the Church's witness has been undermined consistently by unedifying and unpleasant conflicts, alienating people both from its fellowship and its message, as a number of recent high-profile cases have illustrated all too clearly.

2. Spiritual

As Christians we have a great deal to gain by enjoying fellowship, learning from one another and working together for God's kingdom. Psalm 133 dates from the time when brothers would frequently live together in order to preserve an inheritance. It was self-evidently of benefit to the whole family if they were able to do so harmoniously! If they failed in this, the family's prosperity and future might well be threatened. But while the Psalm may have originated as a 'Wisdom' poem, its inclusion in the Psalter indicates that it was seen to have a wider application for all God's people, regarded as a family, then as later.

Paul makes a similar point in Colossians 3:15, where he encourages his readers to 'let the peace of Christ rule in your hearts, to which indeed you were called in the one body'. Their former way of living had included behaviour destructive of relationships – anger, rage, malice, slander and abusive language – but these 'clothes' had been taken off, to be replaced by compassion, kindness, humility, meekness and patience. All these heal divisions, build up fellowship and enable co-operation. Above all, forgiveness and love are to characterise relationships within the Christian community, Christ's peace acting as arbiter in all things. The outcome is seen in the following verses: mutual encouragement in faith, uplifting worship, thankful hearts, and positive family relationships. This is no mere 'counsel of perfection'. No doubt the Colossians fell short of this standard from time to time, just as our own Churches and fellowships do. Being human, Christians are likely to disagree with each other on all kinds of issues, but that is no excuse for not striving towards the practical expressions of unity Paul describes here. As well as this passage and the one we have already noted in 1 Corinthians 1, he makes the same point in a number of other letters, encouraging the Christians at Ephesus to 'make every effort to maintain the unity of the Spirit in the bond of peace' (Ephesians 4:1-16); those in Galatia 'through love to become slaves to one another' (Galatians 5:13-15); and the Church in Rome to 'welcome one another, just as Christ has welcomed you, for the glory of God' (Romans 15:7). There is no reason to suppose that twentieth-century Christians need this teaching any less – it could be argued that many of the Church's problems throughout its history have been the result of ignoring it!

3. *Practical*

The advantages of working together co-operatively are clear enough, whether or not the context is Christian, and in the present economic climate it makes good practical sense to share resources and expertise. However, these should be seen as a by-product of Christian Unity, not a motivation for it.

OVERCOMING THE OBSTACLES

The Church has frequently been criticised for not adapting quickly enough (or at all) to changes in the world and society. Just as frequently, it has been condemned for trying to make those changes. But while most attempts to bring about change in some aspect of the Church's life meet with opposition at some point, those seeking to break down traditional denominational barriers have attracted rather more than the average level of hostility. So, before setting out down the ecumenical path, every Church should take account of the kind of objections likely to be encountered:

1. *'We've got enough to do keeping our own Church going – everyone's already at full stretch. There's no time for anything extra.'*
This is a line of argument which may arouse initial sympathy. Many Churches do struggle to stay afloat, and often rely heavily on a few very committed souls putting in a great deal of time and energy. However, the two underlying assumptions behind this objection are that engaging in Christian worship and service with members of other Churches is of secondary importance, and likely to take up excessive time.

The latter point can be knocked on the head fairly simply, because working with other Christians may well enable things to be achieved by combining resources which would not have been possible otherwise – it might even *save* time and effort! (One might add that overloading a few willing 'pack horses' is itself a counterproductive and ineffi-

cient way of running a Church). The first point is really to do with priorities. Sadly, too many Churches still regard self-preservation as more important than breaking down barriers and building relationships, so that even in the context of ecumenical discussions the emphasis will fall on differences of style rather than our common faith and mission. But if the priority is to proclaim the kingdom of God and make disciples (with which few Christians would argue), those differences will themselves be secondary to the overriding common aim.

2. *'I'm proud of being Anglican. If I'd wanted to be a Methodist, I'd have joined their Church instead.'*
If critical remarks are anything to go by, many worshippers are obviously less proud of their own Churches than this speaker! However, the music behind the words of this comment is really that familiar old tune, 'I'm used to doing it my way'. We all become accustomed to a particular style of worship, assume that God prefers it that way, and baulk at the first sign of change. But we forget that not everyone sees things as we do, and by digging our heels in we not only alienate others and create divisions, but also miss out on opportunities to learn and grow in the Christian life. God is far less concerned about our denominational or structural allegiance than he is about our spiritual life and willingness to love and serve him.

3. *'Anglicans are more concerned with ritual and forms of words than with real faith.'*
Despite all the progress of the past thirty years there are still far too many false assumptions about other Christian traditions, most of which have little basis in fact. Some Churches are genuinely afraid of having fellowship with believers who may not share all their perspectives, while others see any ecumenical venture simply as an opportunity to convert others to their own cause. However, few congregations are monochrome. On the contrary, most contain a wide variety of different viewpoints, and trying to label them rarely conveys the reality – it usually gives a very misleading impression, both of the tradition and the individual members. Once links of fellowship are established and nurtured, such false assumptions tend to die away in time, though this requires perseverance.

4. *'We'll end up losing our identity and distinctiveness.'*
Our identity as human beings is bound up with those we relate to day by day – our families, school friends, work colleagues or neighbours in the community. For Christians the Church family is just as important, fulfilling a spiritual need to belong both to God and to a community of other believers. The identity of that community is often inextricably linked with the way things have always been done, and what it represents. LEP covenants have written-in safeguards to ensure the identity and integrity of the participating traditions. Their effectiveness is based on each participant accepting the traditions of the others, and feeling valued for the contribution they bring. The aim should never be to reduce everything to a lowest common denominator. Having said that, there's 'no gain without pain', and the occasional loss of an evening service, for example, may be necessary if the benefits of interdenominational worship are to be experienced. Some LEPs have gone so far as to establish their own new liturgical tradition, particularly in places where a new church has been set up from scratch.

5. *'United Services are so dull. I get nothing out of them. I'd much rather stay at home and watch TV.'*
It's true that some ecumenical services are extremely boring – but then, sadly, so are plenty of others I've attended. What a tragedy! Worship should never, ever be boring. After all, it's what we were created for, the most important thing we can ever do, and the nearest we'll come to heaven during this life! Part of the problem lies within the comment itself. We don't attend a church service in order to get something out of it, as though it were another consumer product. Instead we bring the worship of our hearts day by day, along with other Christians, to offer to God the very best we can of ourselves. Seen from this perspective a service is only as boring as the people present. To be fair, some of the ecumenical worship I've shared in has been far more stimulating, challenging, entertaining and worthwhile than the vast majority of TV programmes. Hopefully, by reading this book, you'll create ecumenical worship so attractive that nobody will even want to stay in and watch TV!

57 VARIETIES?

Ecumenical worship and activity come in a wide range of forms and styles – even LEPs vary greatly according to local circumstances. Frequently the partnership will have started with an occasional one-off worship event, which may then develop into a regular programme of services through the year. These usually take place in different churches on a rota basis, organised either by the host congregation or by a co-ordinating group made up of representatives of the different traditions. A further development might be some kind of social or community project undertaken together, which is commissioned and supported by an occasional act of worship. This kind of service usually bears the liturgical hallmarks of the church in which it takes place.

In some places these local relationships have developed into something much more cohesive – the Local Ecumenical Partnership. Some of the earliest examples came about in new towns and housing developments, where local Christians intentionally started to worship across denominational boundaries. Since then a variety of circumstances have caused groups of local Churches to formalise a developing relationship by signing a 'covenant' together, committing themselves to regular and continuing joint worship and service to the community. This sort of 'covenant partnership' will not necessarily involve shared worship every Sunday, but there are a growing number of 'Church partnerships' in which Churches of different traditions share the same building, the same ministry team, or even become one congregation. As a result, ecumenical worship is moving on from experiencing and acknowledging a different liturgical tradition, leading to new approaches being sought and created in many instances. There is a wealth of resources available in all the traditions, both recently published and well proven over the years. However, these are designed for general use, and may not always be suitable for addressing specific local issues and concerns.

SETTING OFF ON THE RIGHT TRACK . . .

In a Lent study group a couple of years ago were two gentlemen who shared the same name, but in most other respects were complete opposites. One had been brought up with the richness of the Anglo-Catholic tradition and preferred worship to be very formal, with as much tradition and ritual as possible. The other had been a Methodist from childhood, and was much happier with the unadorned simplicity of the non-conformist chapel. Thankfully both were open enough to learn a great deal from each other. Differences of taste are inevitable in any group of human beings and Christians are no exception: some like the English Cathedral tradition of music, while others would choose a rock band; some like intercessions which are prepared and read out, others prefer the freedom of spontaneous extempore prayer – apparently some even enjoy a longer sermon! But they soon forget that those outside the Church find the existence of so many different denominations strange, especially when they display reluctance to build co-operative and constructive relationships, let alone join forces in worship or Christian service.

Not everyone is aware of the role history has played in all this, both nationally and locally. The Church of England came into being as a result of a dispute with the Church of Rome, something still not properly resolved nearly five centuries later. In the eighteenth century, with the Church of England generally at a low ebb, Methodism came to the fore as the Wesleys' preaching spoke powerfully to parts of society unreached by the established Church. Links between the Anglican and Methodist Churches are certainly stronger, but even after two hundred years they are not yet to be fully restored. At the local level one Church may well see itself traditionally as standing in a different camp from the Church down the road – indeed, in some places Churches were established specifically to express disagreement with another local Church. At its most extreme this cautious attitude can become utterly destructive.

These inbuilt difficulties are enough to overcome, but some attempts to establish ecumenical partnerships have compounded them with an ill-considered approach. The motivation may have been commendable, but the implementation did not achieve what was intended, maybe because of a lack of awareness of the issues involved, or because enthusiasm outran realism. At the opposite extreme, other efforts have recognised this potential pitfall and opted for extensive consultation and discussion before moving forwards, leading to the whole process becoming bogged down in a morass of meetings and discussions. The first casualty in both cases will be good and attractive worship. So, before investigating the possibilities of ecumenical worship, the first task is to establish a secure foundation for it:

1. Be honest and realistic about the past, and how people feel about it. Has there been a history of conflict or suspicion between any of the Churches involved? Were any of them created by splitting away from another Church? Even within a denomination Churches may not see eye to eye. If these issues are not brought into the open and addressed it is almost certain that sooner or later they will come to the fore and prevent further progress. In a few extreme cases a public service of reconciliation has been held to bring these to God for healing and forgiveness, before seeking his blessing on the newly forged partnership. Even if this is not felt necessary, a clear statement from Church leaderships that past agendas have been dealt with may be needed to put minds at ease in the congregations concerned.

2. Even where there has been no actual conflict, Churches will not necessarily have a strong or deep relationship. This may be down to differences of emphasis or focus or more regrettably because respective ministers in the past have not seen eye to eye. Some Churches also have a reputation for 'isolationism', either through being too busy with internal matters or because of an in-built suspicion of Christians from a different tradition. In this case relationships are

more likely to be superficial than fractious, and the congregations may feel little need to join in worship with other traditions. There needs to be clear practical commitment on the part of all the participating Churches to whatever proposals are drawn up, with due respect shown to any who have opted out. Without this, ecumenical ventures become marginalised as the preserve of a small band of enthusiasts.

3. In many places there is an increasing willingness on the part of local Church members to put aside denominational differences and barriers and learn to worship and work together as members of God's kingdom. However, alongside the good will and co-operative spirit there are also plenty of false assumptions and unrealistic expectations. It is very important to enable people to learn about and discover each other's traditions of worship, so that they become aware of the reality – experience suggests that many worshippers are fairly clueless about their own liturgical tradition, let alone anyone else's! Without this basic step there is little prospect of Churches moving forward together.

4. There also has to be realism about how much progress can be made, and how quickly. For most of its history the Church has tended to drag its heels and resist change, even when the need for it is blindingly obvious. Many Christians are still inclined to be cautious about anything new or unfamiliar, understandably wanting to avoid jumping on every bandwagon that rolls past, regardless of where it's heading. So although perceptions and attitudes will start to shift, evidence of change isn't likely to appear overnight. Additionally, a large number of very active Church members have many other pressures and demands to cope with, both at work and in the family. They are not going to feel too committed to a whole lot more meetings and events to attend unless they recognise the effort is worth it. Ecumenical worship needs to be well organised and presented if today's busy Christians are to give it high priority.

GETTING THE SHOW ON THE ROAD . . .

Ecumenical worship is essentially no different to any other form, in that its main aim is to worship God our heavenly Father, through his Son Jesus Christ, in the power of the Holy Spirit. While there may be legitimate discussion about the various component parts of the liturgy, there can surely be no disagreement among Christians that this should not undermine or detract from the fundamental purpose. If the music is not to everyone's taste, or the sermon goes on a bit too long for some, it should still be possible for everyone to go home afterwards feeling inspired and challenged, having met with God together.

The differences that can become such a sticking point are generally less to do with purpose, than with style and approach. This applies equally to an occasional 'Churches Together' service and regular worship in an LEP, and even to the so-called 'structural' differences, which separate denominations on an official, organisational level. Certain historical rules therefore remain in force, most of which surround eucharistic worship, especially for those in the Roman Catholic and Anglican Churches – a commendable desire to progress towards eucharistic fellowship at the local level is often frustrated by the inability of ancient structures to accommodate a new, more ecumenical climate. As a result, occasional services involving Churches from a number of different traditions rarely include Holy Communion, particularly if Roman Catholics are to participate, since they are forbidden to receive the bread and wine from anyone other than a Roman Catholic priest. In reality this is often a matter of individual conscience, and many practising Roman Catholics are willing to receive the sacrament in another tradition, though this cannot be officially recognised. Those from a nonconformist tradition (Baptists especially, though not exclusively) may be unwilling to take the wine from a chalice, while some Methodists will not accept alcoholic communion wine. There are also certain anomalies: for example, in law an

Anglican priest is able to preside at a Methodist Holy Communion service, but his Methodist colleague cannot return the compliment. Fortunately, where an LEP is recognised this may be circumvented, and the participating traditions take it in turn to preside at the Eucharist – they may even be able to devise their own ecumenical liturgy.

EXTERNAL INFLUENCES

1. The occasion of the service

The first thing to take into account has to be the occasion of the service. It might be a celebration of one of the great Christian festivals; in contrast it could be a more local event, such as a Church anniversary, or an event in the community. Rather than a celebration, the service might be an act of commitment and dedication (perhaps at the start of Christian Aid week), or even a commemoration (such as Remembrance Sunday). Although many such occasions recur each year, a few will be a one-off response to a particular event – the sad death of Princess Diana provoked many ecumenical vigils and memorial services, while towns and communities which have experienced a local tragedy also express their shared grief across denominational barriers. Whatever the occasion, ecumenical liturgy has to build on common ground, that which exists already, seeking first to draw people together in worship of our one Lord before making a point of giving them a new experience.

2. Music

Music is likely to be a sensitive area. Most traditions have their own hymn book, and while many modern worship songs seem to transcend the denominational divide, an equally large number of Churches now make their own local selection. In any event, what is well known to one congregation may be unknown to another. It should not be assumed that the organ will provide all the accompaniment, since many larger churches have a competent instrumental group (as do some smaller

ones). With sufficient notice it might even be possible to form a 'united choir' or worship group for the service. Areas of responsibility should be very clearly defined, so that opportunities for Christian unity to be disrupted are minimised!

3. Leadership and participation

Another frequent matter for debate is leadership and participation. For occasional acts of worship involving several Churches, the usual pattern is for the host Church to take responsibility for the liturgy, and to offer various elements of it to members of the other participating congregations. Often a guest preacher is invited, or one of the other local ministers will be asked to speak. The very different circumstances of an LEP generally result in liturgical responsibility being alternated between the traditions, though with the Church of England's proviso that eucharistic services not conducted according to Anglican rites or by an ordained Anglican priest are described as 'an ecumenical service . . . in the (Anglican/Methodist/Baptist) tradition'. Serious problems will arise in the area of leadership and responsibility for ecumenical worship if one Church is allowed to dominate the proceedings by virtue of its size or influence, or because it is not prepared to accommodate the views and sensitivities of others. Likewise, a Church leader with a powerful personality or strongly expressed preferences can cause similar resentment and irritation, and the eventual withdrawal of participation by others in the group may result if the problem is not addressed.

4. Worship and the use of ritual and symbol

Some agreement is vital over the style of worship and the use of ritual and symbol, (this will not necessarily go along denominational lines – some Roman Catholics find the more Catholic elements of the Church of England surprisingly 'high church', while nonconformist congregations can be more formal in worship than their local parish church). Charismatic worship is as likely to be found in an Anglican setting as in a Baptist one, and the absence of a written liturgy is no guarantee of spontaneity or freedom. While the particular 'flavour' of the host Church will probably come through, there must be a recognition on all sides that the different outlooks and approaches of others should be accepted and respected. This could be seen simply as common courtesy, though fundamentally it is an expression of Christian love. A personal preference for traditional hymns and music should not lead to a wholesale rejection of modern worship songs and an instrumental group, nor should a desire for lively charismatic worship lead to judgement being passed on those whose tastes are less exuberant. Candles, icons or other visual symbols should be seen as having no denominational significance – where used, the reasons should be clear and accepted by all.

SERVICE OPTIONS

1. The first question to be asked in the planning of any ecumenical act of worship is also the most fundamental – will the service be eucharistic? An increasing number of worshippers would love to see the present barriers demolished, but regrettably this is not likely to happen for a while yet, at least on an official basis. However, the problem can be addressed. The biggest concern is accommodating those from the Roman Catholic Church, since they are not allowed to receive the sacrament in any other Christian tradition. Unless a priest is presiding at the Eucharist, the usual solution is for Roman Catholic worshippers to receive a blessing at the altar rail instead – as *Travelling Together** neatly expresses it, 'the pain caused by our not being able to receive Communion together can encourage and goad people to work harder in the search for Christian unity'. There are fewer complications with other denominations, though officially the Church of England does not

Travelling Together, a handbook on Local Ecumenical Partnerships, E. Welch and F. Winfield. Published by Churches Together in England.

recognise the validity of any other eucharistic ministry. In practice, most members of the mainstream denominations will receive the sacrament in another tradition at a one-off occasion, tolerating minor variations in style and language, though regular eucharistic services in an LEP need to be organised on an agreed rota basis.

2. The next question is about context – why is this ecumenical service being held at this particular time? There are a number of points in the liturgical year which lend themselves particularly well to combined worship. Many services at Christian festivals will be held on a Sunday evening for practical reasons, though it makes a stronger case for unity when Churches are willing to combine their main morning worship in order to express Christian unity more visibly.

There are other specifically Christian occasions when churches may recognise the value and importance of coming together in worship. One member Church may have reached an important anniversary, for example, or there may be a joint local initiative in mission and evangelism. The Week of Prayer for Christian Unity, Christian Aid Week and One World Week are all local reflections of wider national ventures now usually tackled ecumenically, and there are a number of occasions (the Women's World Day of Prayer being a well-known example) which are explicitly ecumenical in intent and planning. Nor should it be forgotten that many Church members are increasingly familiar with other Christian traditions through taking part in non-denominational events such as Spring Harvest.

Local celebrations and occasions can also motivate Churches to unite in worship. Often it will be something positive, such as a service which forms part of a civic festival or those which celebrated the new Millennium; however, it may be more sombre, for example the anniversary of a tragedy like Hillsborough. The start of the Gulf War and the death of Princess Diana were national occasions when traditional denominational barriers were broken down, at least temporarily, as people sought a spiritual expression for their feelings of anxiety or distress.

3. The third question concerns scale – how many Churches are expected to be involved, and how many people are likely to be present? Complexity and the need for careful preparation increase as numbers go up! The building to be used is a significant factor, too, as it may well put constraints on what you would like to do. However desirable it may be for each Church to take it in turn to host ecumenical worship, the occasion is not likely to be a success if two hundred people are crammed into a building designed for half that number, each taking it in turn to breathe! On the other hand, a smaller number using a very large building might feel they are rattling around somewhat in an atmosphere hardly conducive to worship. With a smaller congregation it may be possible to use existing hymn- or service-books, whereas a major event will probably require a specially produced service-sheet. If the Eucharist is to be celebrated, or the congregation are going to be out of their seats and moving around at any point (e.g. for the Peace or some other ritual act), bear in mind that with larger numbers this requires careful 'stage management' if the service is not to take rather longer than anticipated.

4. The fourth question is about atmosphere – will the service be celebratory or penitential, festive or sombre, exuberant or reflective, reassuring or challenging, formal or informal? To some extent this will be determined by external influences, but the biggest single factor will undoubtedly be the way in which the act of worship is planned and led. On occasion it will be right to maintain the same 'feel' throughout, but the majority of services will probably move from one mode to another as they progress. Choice of suitable hymns and liturgical material is the first step, and there is a balance to maintain between familiar and unfamiliar, one tradition and another, and not least between different styles and expectations of worship. At this point it would be all too easy to shirk the challenge and stick with what is known to everyone and 'safe', but while this is effective at minimising complaints, it is not likely to excite or challenge those present. Hymns and prayers should be chosen which are not only appropriate to the theme or time of year, but also extend the horizons of those present and take them forward in their journey of faith. Initially, host Churches will tend to use the liturgies to which they are most accustomed, but as relationships deepen and confidence grows, it is possible to move on to a more integrated approach, concentrating on theme and purpose. The same comments apply to the actual handling of the service. The temptation is to be 'politically correct' in ecclesiastical terms, so that no one is offended, but ecumenical worship will only grow and deepen as people are challenged and strengthened in their faith.

5. The last question is one of style – how can ritual and symbolic actions be incorporated, in order to emphasise the theme and draw worshippers together? Across most mainstream Christian traditions there is now a wide acceptance of drama, mime and dance as a means of communicating the Gospel. Use of these is unlikely to be controversial except with the most conservative, but it is vital that those engaging in them are well practised and rehearsed. Poorly presented, they will simply become a source of embarrassment for both performers and onlookers. Whatever the level of available resources, they should not be stretched beyond their capacity – a simple dramatic sketch done well has much greater impact than an over-ambitious one that falls apart. While suggestions are made in some service outlines about where they might be incorporated into the liturgy, the material used has to be selected locally and tailored to the particular context. The same comments apply to poetry, which needs to be suitable to the theme and meaningfully read.

Other symbols and actions, both traditional and more innovative, are described in greater detail. These are examples of what might be done in a fairly typical situation, but they don't preclude other creative ideas you may have. Where used, it is essential to make sure they are recognised and accepted by everyone involved, and not given any specific denominational significance.

Christians of all denominations are also discovering the benefits of quieter, more reflective worship in the Celtic or Taizé traditions; both are ecumenical in origin and motivation, but beyond the 'feel-good factor' they may provide, both are committed to living out the Gospel in engagement with the real world. Escapism is not an option for Christians, and ecumenical worship offers a great opportunity to challenge God's people to commit themselves to discipleship and costly service.

RESOURCES

There is now an astonishing variety of resources for worship on the market. Many of the mainstream denominations have been producing new liturgies over the last few years. At the time of writing the new *Methodist Worship Book* is hot off the press, while the Church of England has already published some of its new *Common Worship* material, and much more is due to appear in the near future. In addition to *Lent, Holy Week and Easter*, *The Promise of His Glory* and *Patterns for Worship**, which are officially recognised by the Church of England, there are other books of material specifically designed for Anglican liturgy, and many Anglican prayer books from around the world, which bring fascinating and stimulating insights from other cultural backgrounds – those from Kenya and New Zealand are well worth investigating, for example.

Most denominations now make use of the Revised Common Lectionary, and a great deal of material has been produced by the major Christian publishing houses to fit in with this, designed for wide usage and particularly suited to ecumenical worship. The Celtic Christian tradition has seen considerable growth recently, due not least to the excellent material produced and published by the Iona Community, while the prayers written by Lindisfarne's David Adam are also deservedly popular. There are Taizé publications, some from the Benedictine and Franciscan traditions, and an increasing number aimed specifically at children and young people. There has been an explosion of hymns, songs and liturgical music in the last two decades, together with an increased willingness to cross over previous boundaries and combine the hymns and songs of Graham Kendrick, John Bell and John Wesley in the same volume. John Rutter has been in the forefront of an increase in accessible and worshipful music for choirs, and the Royal School of Church Music provides an excellent range of resources and help to Churches across all traditions.

Inevitably not all of this material is even in quality, and in any event it will suit some situations and temperaments more than others. However, much of it is very good indeed and flexible enough to be used in a variety of ways and contexts. Combined with careful selection and planning, there is no reason for any ecumenical act of worship to be dull and stifling, or lacking in richness, variety and challenge.

HOW TO USE THIS BOOK . . .

. . . in three words: flexibly, creatively and prayerfully. It covers a number of different contexts in which ecumenical worship might take place, and provides suggestions for making good use of the opportunities these bring. There is some original worship material, ideas for suitable hymns*, music† and readings, and in one or two instances a sermon outline based on these, together with indications as to other sources of material which might be relevant. Congregational and responsory prayers are indicated throughout by the use of bold type.

* Suggestions for hymns and songs are drawn from *Hymns Old and New (New Anglican Edition)* and *The Source*, both published by Kevin Mayhew, but can be found in most modern hymn books.

† Suggestions for choral music are drawn from the lists of Kevin Mayhew Publishers, and also from the catalogue of music available from the Royal School of Church Music.

* Published by Church House Publishing. Also available on CD: *Visual Liturgy*.

Although the term 'minister' is used to denote the person leading the service, most traditions now accept that the person leading does not need to have been ordained first – lay leadership of worship has long been valued by non-conformists, and ever-reducing numbers of ordained clergy have led to its acceptance in many other Churches. Much of the suggested material has been proved to work in practice, but it needs to be adapted to other circumstances – it is designed to be used flexibly, and in the worship of our Creator God, creatively*. Equally, try using it in the context of personal prayer as you prepare, so that it isn't just another resource to trawl through for 'something a bit different', but enables Christian people to come closer to God as they worship him together across the various traditions, and to commit themselves to serving his kingdom.

The services have been constructed as blueprints, but local circumstances may demand that only some of the material is used, or that it comes in a different sequence. If so, adapt it as necessary!

THE CHRISTIAN YEAR

OVERVIEW

For those less well acquainted with the history of the Church it may well come as something of a surprise to discover that the various denominations have a wide variety of approaches to their celebration of the Christian year. Recognition of Easter, Christmas and Pentecost is more or less universal in some form, and more recently observance of Lent has found its way into most non-conformist Churches through the growth of ecumenical study groups. Mothering Sunday, Harvest Festival and Remembrance Sunday are also generally acknowledged, if with varying amounts of ritual and enthusiasm. Anglican senior citizens will be familiar with 'days of holy obligation', the Christian festivals when they were expected to attend church (highlighted in the new lectionary as 'principal feasts'). Of these, Ash Wednesday, Maundy Thursday, Good Friday and Ascension Day are celebrated by Anglican and Roman Catholic churches, and are also familiar to most non-conformist traditions. Epiphany and All Saints' Day are frequently observed on the nearest Sunday, and there is a growing recognition of the potential of All Saints' Day as an alternative to the secular Hallowe'en festivities. However, the feasts of the Presentation and the Annunciation tend to feature rather less widely.

There is common ground here between all the mainstream Churches, and thus plenty of scope for ecumenical services. The majority of Churches keep their celebration of Easter and Christmas Days 'in-house' unless they are part of an LEP, but Advent and Lent offer a variety of possibilities for worship which cut across the usual demarcation lines. Advent Sunday itself, falling at the start of the Christian year, could be celebratory or reflective, while the 'sharing of the light' has a special resonance in an ecumenical context. Advent is also generally accepted as a time of preparation for Christmas, though as it progresses inexorably towards its festive climax there is a gradual (or in some places rapid) crescendo of carol singing accompanied by mince pies and mulled wine! Christingle and carol services are relatively straightforward to organise ecumenically since their format and content are fairly standard in all traditions, but a quieter, more meditative service offers considerable attractions at a time of year otherwise dominated by the sounds of the consumer society in full flow. The period after Christmas often feels like an anticlimax, and church attendance drops away somewhat, but this can be turned to advantage as a time for reflection on the meaning of the incarnation. Epiphany brings Christmastide to a close, turning our minds towards the life and ministry of Jesus; at the same time it gives the opportunity for Christians to rededicate themselves to serving of God's kingdom at the start of a new year. The annual Covenant Service is an important Methodist tradition around this time, which is increasingly being opened up to members of other Churches and valued greatly by all who share in it.

In many areas Lent study and discussion groups are now widely accepted as one of the year's major ecumenical events. They could be launched on Ash Wednesday or the first Sunday in Lent with a reflective and penitential service, and brought to a close on Palm Sunday as members of the groups come together to share their reflections and Lenten journey, and prepare for Holy Week and Easter. Holy Week can also work well across the different traditions. A Good Friday Walk of Witness is also now familiar as an act of witness shared by local Christian churches, generally concluding with a short time of worship, and some churches, especially those in LEPs, also share more extended united worship.

The next major festival after Easter is Ascension Day, a great excuse to offer praise and worship to the risen and ascended Christ, while Pentecost reminds us that we are one in the Spirit and commits us afresh to Christian unity in the power of the Spirit. Much later in the year comes All Saint's Day, which enables Christians to look back at God's people in past generations and be challenged by their example. It is also now commonly used as an alternative to the secular Hallowe'en, with Churches joining forces, sharing resources, and coming together for a lively, family-orientated act of worship followed by a party, this being the right time of year for fireworks!

Mothering Sunday and Harvest Festival can also be considered for their ecumenical potential. The former emphasises that all Christians are members of God's family, whatever their tradition, and with sensitivity can be used to reinforce the Christian concept and understanding of family life. The latter could be used as part of a local initiative to help those in need, and to underline how all Christians can play a part in meeting the desperate needs of three-quarters of the world's population.

ADVENT SUNDAY

The Church's two greatest festivals, Christmas and Easter, are both preceded by a period of penitence. Lent was traditionally a time during which baptismal candidates were prepared for their baptism on Easter Day, and was probably observed long before the Churches fixed the date of Christmas. Once the Western Churches had fixed their celebration of Christ's birth on 25 December (probably taking over an existing pagan festival), it too acquired a time of preparation, which became known as Advent. While the primary focus of this was to look forward to the incarnation of our Lord, it soon also became a time for rejoicing in his promise to return one day in glory as King of kings. A further Advent theme is light, particularly appropriate as the days become shorter, symbolised by the lighting of the candles on the Advent wreath. The combination of all these makes for one of the richest seasons of the liturgical year, one which is sadly often neglected as Christmas preparations become ever more frantic.

An evening act of ecumenical worship could have no better start than the sharing of the light by all members of the congregation. Apart from the altar candles (or one main candle in a non-conformist church) there should be no other lights on, other than one or two where necessary to prevent accidents. If possible the congregation should assemble at the back of the church, each holding an unlit candle with a drip shield. One representative then lights a taper from the main candle and brings it to the

minister, who uses its light to read a short welcome and bidding. The light is then shared around until everyone has returned to their seat with a lighted candle. If there is not enough space for everyone to gather, invite a few representatives of each participating Church to do so while everyone else remains in their place. These representatives then share their light with the rest of the congregation, who can pass it along each row. If there is an Advent wreath, one candle should already be lit – though this would not make sense as part of the liturgy unless the Churches intended to worship together on each of the four Sundays of Advent.

Some Churches, especially if they have a competent choir, will want to sing the Advent Prose, which emphasises corporate judgement rather than personal wrongdoing. If used, this should precede the bidding and sharing of light – but make sure the choir can see their scores! Since Advent is a penitential season, it is particularly apt to include a confession that all can share in, however brief.

Another traditional way of marking Advent is to use the hymn *O come, O come, Emmanuel* in its original form as a series of 'antiphons', with the readings on which each verse is based read out first, followed by a prayer and response. Since the hymn is familiar to most traditions, it is unlikely that this approach would be associated with a particular denomination, and it serves to highlight the Advent themes.

A reading traditionally associated with Advent Sunday is from the later verses of Matthew 25, in which Jesus describes how God will pass judgement on the 'great day of the Lord'. The emphasis is clearly on acts of compassion and practical caring as an expression of faith. It is now increasingly common for Churches to use Advent as an opportunity to support a Christian charity, usually aimed at relieving need or providing something to make Christmas more worthwhile. Some collect shoeboxes filled with toys and sweets; others will collect money. In my own local area, the Churches Together group put on 'Christmas Alone', a Christmas Day lunch for those who'd otherwise spend the day on their own. Whatever is done, an Advent Service is the ideal occasion to ask God's blessing on the venture.

ADVENT SERVICE

The Bidding

We are a chosen people,
a people belonging to God,
who has called us out of darkness
into his wonderful light.
In his name we come together
to celebrate once again
the coming of God's Kingdom among us,
and to wonder afresh
at the mystery of his loving purposes for us.

Let us confess our sins and failings to God
in penitence and faith:
words spoken without sensitivity;
actions lacking in compassion;
attitudes rooted in selfishness.
May we seek his pardon
for our divisions and disunity,
our failure to live in his light,
and receive with joy his forgiveness and peace.

Silence

Let us listen with open ears and minds
to the good news of God's kingdom
and receive it into our hearts and lives.
May we gladly celebrate
the birth of our Saviour,
and willingly respond to the message
of peace on earth
and goodwill to all people.

Silence

Let us commit ourselves anew
to serving God faithfully
as we pray for those in need –
the vulnerable and exploited,
the anxious and fearful,
the unloved and lonely,
the grieving and hopeless.
May we demonstrate in our lives
the reality of God's love
as seen in Jesus Christ,
and reflect the justice and peace
of his kingdom.

Silence

Let us express the Christian hope
of eternal life in our praise and worship,
as we remember those
who have gone before us
in the faith of Christ;
as we serve him day by day
in the power of his Spirit;
as we look forward with confidence
to that day when we will see him
face to face.

Silence

Lord, guide us in the ways of peace,
lead us in your righteousness,
and set our hearts on fire with love for you,
now and for ever.
Amen. Come, Lord Jesus.

The sharing of the light

Jesus said,
'I am the light of the world.
Whoever follows me
will not walk in darkness,
but have the light of life'.

As each person passes the light to another:
The light of Christ
As each person receives the light from another:
Thanks be to God.

During this, a Taizé chant could be sung softly;
'The Lord is my light' (HON 486) is especially
suitable.

Hymn

Make way, make way (HON 329) or
Thou, whose almighty Word (HON 514)

Confession and absolution

We bring all our sins to Christ,
the Light of the World,
confessing them openly and honestly.

Lord Jesus,
you call us to be good stewards
but often we fail you.
You call us to use your gifts
for the wellbeing of others,
but we stockpile them
for our own comfort.

**You call us to show compassion
to the stranger and the prisoner,
but we think only of our own interests.
You call us to be merciful to others
as you are merciful to us,
but we harbour resentment and jealousy
in our hearts.
We repent of our sins and wrongdoing
and ask you to forgive us.
Strengthen us to serve and obey you,
and prepare our hearts
for the day of your coming in glory. Amen.**

May God in his mercy
pardon and cleanse us,
keep us faithful in his service,
and make us ready to stand before him
and hear him say 'Well done',
through Jesus Christ our Lord. Amen.

Hymn

O come, O come, Emmanuel (HON 358)

*The following readings are associated with each of
the commonly sung verses of this hymn, and could
be read in between them:*
Isaiah 11:1-4 ('O come, thou Rod of Jesse . . .')
Numbers 24:15b-17 ('O come, thou Dayspring
. . .')
Isaiah 22:21-23 ('O come, thou Key of David . . .')
Exodus 3:1-6 ('O come. O come, thou Lord of
Might . . .')

The Promise of His Glory also contains a short
prayer after each of these, to which the congregation
responds*: **Amen. Lord, have mercy.**

* Published by Church House Publishing. Also available
on CD: *Visual Liturgy.*

Reading

Isaiah 52:7-10

Hymn

How lovely on the mountains (HON 219)

Reading

Romans 13:11-14

Anthem

There is probably as much music for church
choirs to sing at Advent and Christmas as
there is for the rest of the year! Choice of
material will depend largely on the standard
of the singers and the amount of time available for rehearsal, though the anthems
beloved of Anglican choirs won't always sit
easily in a multi-denominational setting. One
of the following choral pieces would be
effective as part of an Advent Sunday act of
worship with a choir drawn from the participating churches:

4-part anthems:
'O thou the central orb' (Wood)*
Favourite Anthem Book 1
'How beauteous are their feet' (Stanford)
favourite Anthem Book 4
'Light of the world' (Elgar)
Favourite Anthem Book 8
'The shepherd' (Mawby)
Twelve Sweet Months
'Great Father of light' (Mawby)
Fourteen New Anthems

* Also available in 3-part settings in *Favourite Anthem
Book 3.*

Reading

Matthew 25:31-46

Hymn

Heaven shall not wait (HON 207)

Address or meditation

Song

You are the King of Glory (HON 570)

Intercessions

Creator God,
you made this world out of nothing
and saw that all of it was good.
How it must grieve you
to see how we have abused and spoiled
its riches and beauty!
We pray for those who work to look after it
and ensure its resources
are distributed more fairly among all people.

Father in heaven,
Hear our prayer.

Emmanuel, God with us,
you came to share our human life
that we might share your eternal life.
How you must weep
over the bitterness and hatred,
the selfishness and lack of care
which afflict our society.
We pray for those
on the margins of the community:
the lonely and unloved,
the homeless and helpless,
the abused and vulnerable,
the anxious and depressed.

Father in heaven,
Hear our prayer.

Holy Spirit, Comforter and Enabler,
you are the presence of God within us,
our conscience, encourager and guide.
How you long for us to be more open
to your teaching and leading!
We pray for your Church throughout the world,
and especially here in . . . ,
that we may be united in worship and witness,
and dedicate ourselves
to bringing the light of Christ
to all whom we meet.

Father in heaven,
Hear our prayer.

Holy and loving God,
fill us with joy and hope
as we work for the coming of your kingdom
and look forward to that day
when we will see you face to face,
through Jesus Christ our Lord. Amen.

Our Father . . .

Hymn

Hills of the north, rejoice (HON 209) or
We will cross every border (Source 560)

Final prayer

Come among us
and dwell with us, Lord Jesus.

Come and bring light
to dispel our darkness.
Come and bring hope
to drive out our fear.
Come and bring joy
to banish our sorrow.
Come and bring love
to fill our longing hearts,
that through us the whole world
may come into your light. Amen.

Blessing

May God our Father,
the Creator and Sustainer of all,
give us a fresh vision of his kingdom.
Amen.

May Christ his Son,
the Saviour and Redeemer of all,
cleanse us from all sin
and open up for us
the way of eternal life.
Amen.

May his Holy Spirit
fill us with divine love,
empower us to live for his glory,
and make us ready
for the day of his coming.
Amen.

Hymn

Lo, he comes with clouds descending
(HON 307) or
Lord, the light of your love (HON 317)

A REFLECTIVE SERVICE FOR ADVENT

It may not be practical to organise a large-scale ecumenical event in the weeks leading up to Christmas, but there are likely to be Christians in any area who would welcome the possibility of worship on a smaller and quieter scale. The following service outline would work well for the evening of the second Sunday in Advent (often the one on which

Churches are least likely to have a major event planned), but if that is not feasible, it would work just as well on a weekday evening. The weeks of Advent are usually full of all-singing, all-dancing worship spectaculars, but a time for quiet reflection and meditation can be just as effective – some may find it more attractive! As with all ecumenical activities, the presence and support of clergy and ministers will lend a certain weight to the occasion, but there is no reason why this kind of service should not be led by a competent lay person – the ordained ones might even welcome it!

Introduction

When the Lord comes he will banish all darkness, revealing the deepest secrets of our hearts. He knows everything, and we can hide nothing from his searching gaze. Let us quietly prepare our hearts to meet with him in worship.

Silence

Song

On Jordan's bank the Baptist's cry (HON 401)

Prayer of approach

Almighty God,
we stand before you as our judge,
recognising our sinfulness and failings.
Nothing we have ever done
or could possibly do
would make us worthy
to come into your presence.
Yet we stand before you, too,
as our loving Father,
who longs for us to respond
to his gracious invitation.
As we reach out to you,
touch us with your gentle hand,
enfold us in your strong arms,
and reassure us of your love,
for the sake of your Son,
Jesus Christ our Lord. Amen.

Responsive words of praise

The Lord says: Go up to a high mountain
and announce the good news;
**the Lord our God will come
with great power.**

Lift up your voice with strength;
the Lord our God will come to bring justice.

Take the good news to the city;
**the Lord our God will come
to bring salvation.**

Speak tenderly to God's people;
the Lord our God will come to bring comfort.

The Lord says: Do not be afraid,
but lift up your voice,
for I will make a straight path
through the desert;
I will make every hill and mountain low;
and I will make the rough places
smooth and level.
**The glory of the Lord will be revealed
to all people
and they will see it together.**
(from Isaiah 40)

First reading

Malachi 3:1-5

Song

Purify my heart (HON 428)

Second reading

John 1:19-27

Meditation

People in Jesus' day had a variety of theories about who he was – one of the prophets, or even *the* Prophet, perhaps? A wise teacher; a potential revolutionary leader; a healer with 'magical' powers; or maybe a complete charlatan? They needed someone who would show them who Jesus was, how he fitted in with the Old Testament scriptures, and what his ministry would be. That was John the Baptist's role, not to attract attention to himself or to his own life and teachings, but to prepare the way for the coming of Jesus, our Lord and Saviour. As job descriptions go, it was hardly glamorous, and didn't offer much in the way of self-fulfilment, let alone power and influence. But it meant that many were able to get past the speculation about Jesus and encounter his transforming love for themselves.

The same is just as true today. There are any number of ideas in circulation about who Jesus was, what he said and meant, what his significance really was. The calling of God's people is to prepare the way for him to come and bring his love and compassion, his justice and righteousness to a confused and fragmented world. The Church has too often sought the wrong kind of attention – people may be superficially impressed with spectacle and structures, but they may well be distracted from the only reason the Church exists, to proclaim the good news about Jesus, our Emmanuel, God with us.

How might we play our part in preparing the way?

- through demonstrating Christ's love in our fellowship and witness – disunity and divisions put obstacles in the way rather than opening it up

- through joyful witness to our one Lord and Saviour – though we may have slightly different ways of going about it, we do it for the same reason

- through undertaking together Christlike acts of compassion and care which will reveal his love to those in need

- through working together for peace and justice in society.

Advent response

We prepare for Jesus to come into our lives
as Prophet, Priest and King,
saying: 'Come to our hearts, Lord Jesus';
we make room for you there.

Group A: Come to us as Prophet
to challenge our complacency,
shake us out of our lethargy,
and renew our zeal for your kingdom.

Group B: Cleanse and purify us from all that defiles,
and make us willing to say:
Lord here am I, send me.

Group A: Come to us as Priest
to stand by us in our weakness and need,
and enable us to stand in God's presence.

Group B: Give us confidence
to approach the throne of grace,
and receive mercy and help
in our time of need.

Group A: Come to us as King
to reign in our lives,
and strengthen our commitment
to live as members of your kingdom.

Group B: Make us bold
to uphold your law of love,
and bring your justice and peace
to this needy world.

Come to our hearts, Lord Jesus;
we make room for you there.

Song
Inspired by love and anger (HON 252)

Intercessions

We ask God to reveal to us situations in which we can 'prepare the way' for Christ to come into people's lives, into conflict and anger, anxiety and despair, sadness and sickness . . . (*a time of open intercession follows*).

After each spoken prayer, or group of prayers, the Taizé chant 'O Lord, hear my prayer' (HON 379) could be sung as a response.

Song
When God Almighty came to earth
(HON 545)

Final prayer

As we leave this place to return to our homes,
may your kingdom come into our hearts.

As we go to our places of work and colleagues,
may your kingdom come in our service.

As we live among family and friends,
**may your kingdom come
in our relationships.**

As we mix with people
in the everyday activities of life,
may your kingdom come in our lives.

Looking for God's kingdom to come,
we pray together as he taught:
Our Father . . .

Blessing

In our homes and families
let us bless the Lord.

In work and leisure
let us bless the Lord.

In worship and devotion let us bless the Lord.
Thanks be to God.

THE CHRISTMAS SERVICE

In many Churches the Christmas services are a major highlight of the calendar, with Christingles, carols by candlelight, and cribs dominating the scene. However, strong publicity, hopefully increased attendances, and not least the weight of received tradition mean that Christmas is just about the most difficult time of year to engage in ecumenical worship. The exception to this is found mostly in well-established LEPs, where the people no longer dream of a united Christmas because it has been made to happen. (Our own LEP has reached this stage, though it has taken a couple of years to merge the two traditions into a coherent programme – and we're not sure it's quite right even now!). Ironically, the mainstream Churches have more in common at Christmas than at almost any other time of year, as the carols, readings and symbolism are recognised by everyone.

Christingle and crib services come in more or less the same form in every tradition and are ideally suited to ecumenical worship, even if there are guaranteed to be a few minor differences in execution. The carol service (often entitled a 'Festival of Carols' or 'Carols by Candlelight') is also familiar to all denominations, though it may vary in style from the formal and tightly structured 'Nine Lessons and Carols' (Anglican in origin and style) through to a more lively and exuberant 'Carol Praise'

(in the charismatic tradition). An ecumenical version will probably try to combine the best of both worlds.

From traditional carols to the folk ballads of the Iona Community, from Plainsong to John Rutter or John Taverner, there is a wealth of Christmas music available. What you choose will be determined as much as anything by the available resources. The following outline suggests one way that well-known items can be integrated together by a common thread. Readings 1 and 7 frame the narrative, describing God's eternal purposes, and the rest of the readings and the carols reflect our response to God's love in Christ. A final reading and song express our commitment to what we have heard and understood. Each reading is concluded with a brief prayer, and an opening bidding in modern style is also included, together with a closing response.

Bidding

In the name of our Lord Jesus Christ we welcome you all, as we gather together once more to hear the story of his coming among us as a helpless baby, yet Lord of all. With the shepherds we run joyfully to the manger, to see for ourselves the Word made flesh. With the angels we sing 'Glory to God in the Highest', and join with the praises of all heaven as we celebrate the coming of our Saviour. With the wise men we bring to the infant Christ our own gifts and offerings, to acknowledge him as King of Kings. With Mary and Joseph we ponder these things in our hearts, as we seek to understand more of God's loving purposes.

We offer to God our prayers for the world into which he sent his Son, with its conflict and chaos, its greed and selfishness, its sadness and pain, especially . . .

We offer to God our prayers for the Church throughout the world, divided and confused, yet united in our one Lord and in seeking to bring the good news of his love to all people . . .

We offer to God our prayers for those whose rejoicing at this Christmas season will be overshadowed by grief, illness, anxiety or loneliness, especially . . .

We pray finally for ourselves, that we may not only hear the familiar story of Christ's birth, but may open our minds to reflect on it, our hearts to respond to it, and our lives to proclaim it, day by day. And so we worship the newborn King, together with the angels and all God's people throughout the world, rejoicing at his coming among us and praying as he taught:
Our Father ...

Carol

O come, all ye faithful (HON 357)

First reading

John 1:1-14

Prayer

Living Word,
who came to be the light for all people;
shine in our darkness
and help us to recognise you
living among us,
that believing in your name,
we may become children of God. Amen.

Carol

Of the Father's love begotten (HON 395)

Second reading

Isaiah 11:1-9

Prayer

Lord God,
may your Spirit of wisdom and understanding
rest upon us,
that we may deal fairly with the needy
and act justly for the world's poor. Amen.

Carol

Who would think (God's surprise) (HON 558)

Third reading

Zechariah 2:10-13

Prayer

Lord Jesus,
as you once came to live among your people,
come now and dwell in our hearts,

that we may rejoice and be glad
as your presence breaks into our lives
with power. Amen.

Carol

Lord Jesus Christ (HON 311)

Fourth reading

Luke 1:26-38

Prayer

Lord God,
as we hear your gracious call,
make our ears open to the message you give,
and our hearts willing to obey you
as faithful servants. Amen.

Carol

For Mary, mother of our Lord (HON 136)

Fifth reading

Luke 2:8-14

Prayer

Lord Jesus,
we hear again the angels' song of praise
at your coming to earth as our Saviour;
rejoicing with them,
may we treasure what we see
and hear in our hearts,
that our lives may reflect
the presence of Emmanuel, God with us. Amen.

Carol

Angels from the realms of glory (HON 34)

Sixth reading

Matthew 2:1-12

Prayer

Lord Jesus,
recognising you as King of kings
and Lord of all,
we offer you our gifts
and ask you to use them
for the glory of your kingdom. Amen.

Carol

In the bleak mid-winter (HON 248)

Seventh reading

Hebrews 1:1-4 (or 9)

Prayer

Lord Jesus,
you are the radiance of your Father's glory
and through you the universe was made;
as you descended from your heavenly home
to share our life and bear our sins,
may we make room for you in our hearts
and be filled with your eternal life. Amen.

Carol

Meekness and majesty (HON 335) or
Thou didst leave thy throne (HON 513)

Final reading

Philippians 2:5-11

Carol

From heaven you came, helpless babe
(HON 148)

Final prayer

Lord Jesus,
encouraged by our union with you
and comforted by your love,
make us one in heart and mind.

Lord Jesus,
may we do nothing out of selfish pride
or ambition,
but regard others as more important
than ourselves;
make us one in heart and mind.

Lord Jesus,
may we be filled with your Spirit of humility,
and give priority to the interests of others;
make us one in heart and mind.

Lord Jesus,
may we acknowledge you to be Lord of all,
both with lips which sing your praise,
and in lives dedicated to humbly serving you;

make us one in heart and mind
that together we may confess
that Jesus Christ is Lord,
to the glory of God our Father. Amen.

Carol

Hark, the herald angels sing (HON 199)

Blessing

May God, who in his Son
left heaven's glory to take the form of a servant,
make us faithful in his service.
Amen.

May God, who in his Son
was obedient even to death on a cross,
make us obedient to his perfect will.
Amen.

May God, who has exalted his Son
to the highest place in heaven,
give us grace to acknowledge Christ as Lord
both in word and deed.
Amen.

And the blessing . . .

Choral music

A number of choir anthems could be prepared to fit in with this pattern, either in addition to the carols, or as an alternative. Many of the carols have themselves been set for performance by a choir – the settings found in Carols Old and New *are well worth exploring, and lie easily within the compass of an occasional 'united choir'. Some splendid new settings for choir can be found in* Songs for the Manger *– the 'Charleston Carol', 'See, the Lord of all creation', and 'Peace be yours' are most rewarding to sing.*

The Christmas music of John Rutter is now becoming familiar to a very wide audience, and some of it is available in relatively simple settings – 'Jesus Child', 'Nativity Carol', 'Angels' Carol' and 'Shepherd's Pipe Carol' are all suitable to this outline (though beware the possible 'typo' which led one church to advertise their choir singing the 'Shepherd's Pie Carol'!). Other well-known possibilities include Peter Warlock's 'Bethlehem Down', John Ireland's 'Holy Boy', Herbert Howells' 'A Spotless Rose' and Byrd's 'Hodie Christus natus est'.

Either alternatively or additionally, there are many moving and thought-provoking Christmas poems which would contribute to a formal service like this – John Betjeman's 'Christmas' is a particularly good example.

EPIPHANY

Epiphany rarely feels as celebratory as the rest of Christmas. It marks fairly closely the end of an old year, the end of holidays from school and work, and the end of decorations and celebrations for another eleven months. Perhaps this comes as a relief, but it can also seem a bit of a let-down after all the excitement. For the western Church, Epiphany celebrates the visit of the magi to the infant Christ, and his revelation to the Gentiles. In other Christian traditions the emphasis is on his baptism and the start of his earthly ministry – the Revised Common Lectionary identifies the first Sunday of Epiphany as the feast day for the Baptism of the Lord. Church calendars may make it more practical to use one of the other Sundays of Epiphany for ecumenical activity (Epiphanytide lasts until Candlemas on 2 February), and Christian Unity is a now major theme of this season, since it contains the Week of Prayer for Christian Unity. This is recognised and marked by most mainstream Churches and has a section of its own later in this book.

On an ecumenical level, Epiphany is a great opportunity for a fresh expression of commitment to working more closely together in mission. In many areas the local Churches now unite every few years expressly to bring the good news of Jesus Christ to their community. Since planning for such events invariably takes many months, Epiphany is the ideal point at which to launch a year of mission and evangelism, even though the focal point will probably lie some way ahead.

At this time of year Methodist congregations hold their annual 'Covenant Service', and in some places like to invite members of other Churches and Christian traditions to share in this act of commitment with them, though the Covenant itself could be used in any service which emphasises discipleship and devotion.

Epiphany carol services and processions are the traditional liturgies for this season, though

a major ecumenical celebration in addition to whatever is done during the Week of Prayer for Christian Unity may prove impractical. *The Promise of His Glory** also provides a liturgy for Anglicans to renew their own baptismal promises, though this would be difficult to extend to other traditions with a different view of the sacrament of baptism.

The following outline picks up the themes of revelation and personal commitment to provide a liturgy which can be used by Churches worshipping together at the start of any year, though especially one looking forward to a time of mission and evangelism.

* Published by Church House Publishing. Also available on CD: *Visual Liturgy.*

Opening response

The whole earth is covered
with the darkness of sin and despair.
Arise, shine, for our light has come;
the Lord's glory is rising upon us.

The people of the earth are wandering
in deep darkness and confusion.
Arise, shine, for our light has come;
the Lord's glory is rising upon us.

The nations of the earth will come
to the light of Christ,
their leaders as they see the brightness
of his dawn.
Arise, shine, for our light has come;
the Lord's glory is rising upon us.

Carol

O worship the Lord in the beauty of holiness
(HON 394)

Confession

Lord Jesus Christ,
you reveal your truth to us,
but we fail to understand or obey
your will for our lives.
Forgive our stubbornness;
help us to see your glory.

Lord Jesus Christ,
you reveal your compassion to us,
but we fail to show it to others.

Forgive our selfishness;
help us to see your glory.

Lord Jesus Christ,
you reveal your power to us,
but we prefer to trust our own strength.
Forgive our wilfulness;
help us to see your glory.

Lord Jesus Christ,
you reveal God to us
as Father, Son and Holy Spirit,
perfect in unity,
but we persist in our divisions
and maintain our differences.
Forgive our disunity;
**help us to see your glory,
the glory of the Father's only Son,
and to bear witness to the Word
who became flesh and lived among us,
for his name's sake Amen.**

Absolution

May God in his mercy draw you to himself,
forgive all your sins
and pardon your wrongdoing,
and grant you a vision of his glory,
that through you Christ may be revealed
to all the world,
in whose name we pray.
Amen.

Hymn

Faithful vigil ended (HON 118)

Old Testament reading

Isaiah 49: 6b-13

Psalm

May God be gracious to us and bless us;
Lord, make your face shine upon us.

May God's power be known on the earth;
Lord, show the nations your saving power.

May God be praised by all people;
Lord, let all the peoples praise you.

May the nations be glad and sing for joy;
**Lord, guide them in their ways
and judge them with your righteousness.**

May God bless us
with the riches of his creation;
**Lord, continue to bless us,
that the ends of the earth may honour your
name.**

Let all the peoples praise you, O God,
Let all the peoples praise you. Amen.
(from Psalm 67)

Hymn

God of mercy, God of grace (HON 175)

New Testament reading

1 Peter 2:4-10

Response

How beautiful on the mountains
are the feet of him who brings good news,
proclaiming peace and salvation;
say to the people: 'Your God reigns'.

Burst into songs of joy together,
for the Lord has brought comfort to his people;
say to the people: 'Your God reigns'.

All the ends of the earth will see
the salvation of our God;
say to the people: 'Your God reigns'.

Hymn

How lovely on the mountains (HON 219)

Gospel reading

Matthew 2:1-12

Sermon/Meditation

Procession

The gifts offered could be either twentieth-century equivalents of those offered by the magi, or those which members of the congregation are offering to assist in the mission project which the local Churches are launching. If the former, representatives of three Churches should bring to the altar or Communion table symbolic gold, incense and myrrh. If the latter, invite all members of the congregation to write on a slip of paper what help they might offer to an overall mission event. If each seat

*has a slip of paper on it when people arrive, these
can be collected up by a number of representatives
and presented in the same way, or if necessary
incorporated into the offering. Quiet music could
be played while this happens, or a hymn sung – for
example 'At this time of giving' (HON 47). As
gifts are offered, the following response could be
used:*

Whoever sows generously
will also reap generously.
Thanks be to God for his indescribable gift.

Intercession

With the wise men
we follow the guiding star to Bethlehem,
bringing gifts to offer to Christ our King.
Lord, receive this offering,
and hear our prayers.

Gold speaks of wealth and power,
kingship and government.
We bring to God the nations of the world
and their leaderships,
those who hold high office
in our nation and local community,
those with responsibility for money,
and those in the public eye, especially . . .
May they place in your hands
the influence and resources at their disposal,
to bring relief to the poor and justice to all.
Lord, receive this offering,
and hear our prayers.

Incense speaks of prayer and devotion,
worship and praise.
We bring to God our Churches
both in this local community
and throughout the world,
that Christians may put aside their differences
and through worshipping
and serving God together
demonstrate the unity which Christ has won
for his people.
We pray especially for . . .
May all Christians proclaim your truth
with one voice
and show your love with one heart.
Lord, receive this offering,
and hear our prayers.

Myrrh speaks of suffering and death,
pain and distress.

We bring to God all who are suffering
through ill-health or depression,
anxiety or grief, ill-treatment or exploitation,
mentioning by name . . .
May they know the peace and comfort
of your presence
in their current distress
and the healing touch of your hand.
Lord, receive this offering,
and hear our prayers.

All of our gifts, all of our life
we offer to the infant king.
As he ministers to us
so may we with our gifts
minister his love and compassion
to our world.
This we ask in his name and for his glory.
Amen.

*Alternatively, each bidding can end with '. . . and
hear our prayers', the congregation responding by
using a well-known Taizé chant, e.g. 'In the Lord
I'll be ever thankful' (HON 250) or 'Ubi caritas'
(HON 525).*

Our Father . . .

Song
Let there be love (HON 298)

Final response
We offer to God the worship of our lips
and our lives:
Lord, you have given us this world
and its resources;
make us good stewards
of all you have entrusted to us,
and keep us faithful to our calling.

Lord, you have placed us in families
and communities;
make us good neighbours to those around,
and keep us faithful to our calling.

Lord, in Christ you have forgiven all our sins
of thought and speech, action and inaction;
make us willing to forgive those
who wrong us,
and keep us faithful to our calling.

Lord, you have given us eternal life
and the hope of heaven;
make us faithful witnesses
to the joy of your kingdom,
and keep us faithful to our calling.

Lord, you have called us
to show your limitless love
in acts of service and compassion;
make us worthy servants,
and keep us faithful to our calling.
Accept the worship of our lips and lives,
strengthen us in faith,
and make us one as you are one,
through Jesus Christ our Lord. Amen.

Hymn

From the sun's rising (HON 150)

Blessing

God our Father has called us
from darkness into his wonderful light;
may he shine on our path
and guide our footsteps. Amen.

Jesus Christ his Son is the Light of the World;
may he bring light to our lives
and banish all darkness. Amen.

God the Holy Spirit enlightens our minds
and fills us with his love;
may he shine through our lives
and draw others to the love of God. Amen.

The blessing of God Almighty,
Father, Son and Holy Spirit,
be among us and remain with us
today and always. Amen.
or
The grace of our Lord Jesus Christ,
the love of God,
and the fellowship of the Holy Spirit
be with us all evermore. Amen.

Choral music

Coming at the end of the Christmas season, Epiphany itself can still provide a suitable setting for some of the Christmas anthems, especially those associated with the visit of the magi. Harold Darke's setting of 'In the bleak mid-winter' and Peter Cornelius' 'The three kings' spring immedi-ately to mind, while Carols Old and New has straightforward choral settings of such favourites as 'As with gladness', 'We three kings' and 'The first nowell'. However, there are plenty of options if you prefer to emphasise the themes of mission and evangelism to all people: Handel's great chorus from the Messiah, 'And the glory of the Lord shall be revealed', is particularly appropriate. From Anthems Old and New come Ouseley's 'From the rising of the sun', Stainer's 'How beautiful upon the mountains', or Haydn's 'The heavens are telling'. Among more modern compositions, Colin Mawby's 'Let all the world exultant sing' and Christopher Tambling's 'May none of God's wonderful works keep silence' also fit this theme admirably, both from 30 New Anthems.

A PENITENTIAL SERVICE FOR THE BEGINNING OF LENT

Outside LEPs, where worship is shared already, ecumenical services are frequently organised to celebrate or mark something, be it a Christian festival, an anniversary, or the launch of a joint mission or project. Somehow lively praise and worship seem more suitable for a large gathering of Christians from different traditions than solemnity and reflection, though there are occasional exceptions, such as a major occasion for grief or concern, whether local or national. Being a penitential season, Lent does not therefore immediately come to mind as a time for ecumenical worship. However, in recent years the observation of Lent has spread far beyond the Catholic tradition and entered the ecumenical domain, notably through inter-church study and fellowship groups.

In large groups or small, within our own tradition or in an ecumenical context, we need to take stock of our spiritual life (individual and corporate) and confess to God those areas which need his forgiveness and healing. Lent is a particularly good opportunity to acknowledge the attitudes and behaviour which promote disunity among Christians, and to take a fresh look at how we are progressing with the work of demonstrating and building up our oneness in Christ through worshipping and serving him together. Since Lent groups are now widely accepted in most places, the service outline for the beginning of Lent also provides for these to be launched corporately. At the other end of Lent, Palm Sunday can effectively be used to round them off.

Mention Lent, and many people will immediately think of having to 'give something up' (some older folk may recall being forced to do so). But while it may be very good for us, physically and spiritually, to abandon our usual indulgences of chocolate or alcohol for forty days, that emphasises only the fasting element of Lent. The study groups remind us that Lent originated as a time of spiritual preparation for those who were to be baptised on Easter Day, as well as those who were to be readmitted to the Church after a time of penitence and reflection following some blatant sin. The liturgical emphasis is therefore on looking forward to Good Friday and Easter Day, the heartland of our Christian faith, and something shared by Christians of all traditions. You may feel it helpful to symbolise the 'fasting' aspect by removing any elaborate decor or banners from the church, avoiding flower arrangements, and considering carefully the style of music to be used. However, not all traditions observe Lent in this way, and any changes may need to be explained in advance.

This following outline service is penitential and contemplative in tone, providing an opportunity for the congregation to reflect, respond and look forward to Holy Week and Easter. It includes the imposition of ashes, a practice now widely accepted by Christians from many traditions. However, as some may find this difficult, to avoid offence or misunderstanding you may prefer the alternative approach which is also suggested (see below, page 43).

Opening sentence

The tax collector would not even look up to heaven, but said,
'God, be merciful to me, a sinner'.

Hymn

Dear Lord and Father of mankind (HON 106)

Bidding

Friends, we join together with Christians of all traditions at the beginning of this season of Lent, as we prepare ourselves for the remembrance of our Lord's passion and death, and the celebration of his glorious resurrection. It is a time for personal reflection on our lives; for sorrowing over our sins and honest repentance; for receiving gladly God's promise of forgiveness in Jesus Christ and committing ourselves with fresh resolve to following his way. As we do this in the coming days, we pray that our faith may be strengthened and our devotion deepened.

In our observation of this time of preparation we may spend time in prayer and fasting; we may read and meditate on God's word in the Scriptures; we may discipline ourselves by laying aside familiar comforts in order to focus more clearly on our walk with Christ. We pray now for God's help as we begin our Lenten journey.

Loving God,
we come to you
not knowing how or what to pray,
but bringing you the deepest longings
of our hearts,
which mere words cannot express.
You know our thoughts
before they find shape,
our speech before it comes to our lips,
our intentions before our hands give them form.
Search us this day, O God, and test us,
to remove any wickedness within us
and allay our anxious thoughts.
Give us discernment as we meditate
on your word,
give us peace as we receive your forgiveness,
give us joy as we deepen our life in you,
and lead us in the way of eternal life,
for the sake of your Son,
our Saviour Jesus Christ. Amen.

Response

O Lord my God, I cried to you for help
and you healed me.
Sing to the Lord, and praise his holy name.

Hymn

O for a heart to praise my God (HON 361)

Collect for Ash Wednesday

Old Testament reading

Genesis 2:15-17; 3:1-7 or
Isaiah 1:10-18 or
Joel 2:1-2, 12-17 or
Micah 6:1-8

Responsorial Psalm

Lord, your love never fails.
Be merciful to me
and wipe out all my wrongdoing.
Wash away all our sin,
and make us clean from all that pollutes.

Lord, I know well what I have done wrong,
because my conscience troubles me continually.
We have sinned in your sight,
against you alone;
you are justified in judging us.

Lord, only you can cleanse me
through and through;
make me whiter even than the purest snow.
Do not keep looking at our wrongdoing,
but remove it from sight for ever.

Lord, give me deep within a pure heart
and a right spirit;
uphold me with the presence
of your Holy Spirit.
Bring us back to the joy of your saving love
and keep our spirits willing and generous.

Lord, open my lips to declare your mercy,
and to offer you praise and thanksgiving.
You seek from us the sacrifice of repentance
and brokenness;
you will never despise or turn away
those whose hearts are contrite.

Hymn

Such love (HON 461)

New Testament reading

Romans 5:12-19 or
1 Peter 3:18-22 or
Matthew 6:1-6, 16-21 or
Luke 18:9-14

Sermon

Liturgy of penitence

Jesus says: 'If you obey my commands you will remain in my love.' Aware of our failure to keep them, we listen again to the commandments God has given, that they may be written more clearly upon our hearts.

God says: 'I am the Lord your God.
You are to have no gods other than me.'
Lord, we have not loved you
with all our heart, soul, mind and strength.
Lord, forgive us.

'You shall not make any idol for yourself.'
Lord, we have not worshipped you
in spirit and in truth.
Lord, forgive us.

'You shall not misuse the name
of the Lord your God.'
Lord, we have not worshipped you acceptably,
with reverence and awe.
Lord, forgive us.

'Remember the Lord's Day, and keep it holy.'
Lord, we have not entered
drawn near to you with sincere hearts,
in full assurance of faith.
Lord, forgive us.

'Honour your father and mother.'
Lord, we have not honoured one another,
or looked first to the interests of others.
Lord, forgive us.

'You shall not commit murder.'
Lord, we have not been reconciled
to one another,
nor overcome evil with good.
Lord, forgive us.

'You shall not commit adultery.'
Lord, we have not been pure and blameless
in thought or deed.
Lord, forgive us.

'You shall not steal.'
Lord, we have not been honest in our dealings,
or generous towards those in need.
Lord, forgive us.

'You shall not bear false witness.'
Lord, we have not always spoken the truth
in love.
Lord, forgive us.

'You shall not covet anything
belonging to someone else.'
Lord, we have not always been generous
or willing to share.
**Lord, forgive us,
and write your law of love on our hearts
that we may love you with all our heart
and our neighbour as ourselves.**

Silence

Confession and absolution

God our Father,
you are mighty to save,
but we are weak and sinful,
and have fallen away from your presence.
In your great mercy,
forgive us, O Lord.

God our Father,
you are faithful in every way,
but we are fickle and changeable,
and have put our trust in this passing world.
In your great mercy,
forgive us, O Lord.

God our Father,
you are gracious and forgiving,
but we are critical and self-righteous,
and have not turned to you
in penitence and faith.
In your great mercy,
forgive us, O Lord.

God our Father,
you are eternal and changeless,
but we are earthbound and worldly,
and have not responded
to your forgiving love.
In your great mercy,
forgive us O Lord.

**Wash away our sin and guilt
and help us to see more clearly
what you would have us be,
for the glory of your Son,
our Saviour Jesus Christ. Amen.**

Almighty God,
whose mercy is on all
who sincerely seek his face,
grant you pardon for all your sins,
time to turn to him and repent,
and strength to walk in his way
of peace and freedom,
through Jesus Christ our Lord. Amen.

Imposition of ashes

Prayer before the imposition of ashes

We come to God in penitence and faith,
recognising his holiness and purity,
and conscious of our own unworthiness.
In penitence we now receive
on our foreheads in ash
the sign of the Cross,
to remind us of our need to repent,
and to reassure us of our salvation in Christ.

Holy God,
with these ashes
we acknowledge before you
our sins and failings.
May they be a sign
both of our repentance and our mortality,
and a token of your free gift of eternal life
to all who put their trust in you,
through the death of your dear Son
Jesus Christ. Amen.

Traditionally ashes, formed by burning palm crosses from the previous year, are imposed on penitent worshippers' foreheads by the minister, who has been 'ashed' already by another minister. An increasingly popular alternative to this is for worshippers to impose ashes on each other. These should be placed centrally in a small container on a table. If the former method is chosen, the following response could be used:

Turn away from sin,
and turn to Christ who forgives and restores.
Amen. Lord, have mercy.

In an ecumenical service, with a larger number of worshippers, it may be more appropriate and practical for them to come to the table in twos and make the sign of the cross with the ashes on each other's forehead, with the words:

Repent, and believe the good news.

While this is taking place, a Taizé chant could be sung, either unaccompanied or to a simple melody line from a flute or clarinet. 'Stay with me' (HON 458) or 'Within our darkest night' (HON 562) are particularly suitable.

Prayer after the imposition of ashes

God our loving Father,
you make us for yourself,
and our hearts are restless
until they find rest in you.
Make us pure in thought and motive,
unselfish in word and action
strong in purpose and faith.
May our minds know your will,
our hearts respond to it
and our lives enact it,
for the sake of your Son,
Jesus Christ our Lord. Amen.

Hymn

Give thanks with a grateful heart (HON 154)

Intercessions

Lord Jesus,
you sent your disciples out in twos
to take the good news of God's kingdom
to all whom they met.
We pray for all Christian people
working together for the Gospel,
especially in our own area . . .
Help us to overcome our differences
and show by our actions
that you are our one Lord.
Jesus, Lord of the Church,
in your mercy, receive our prayer.

Lord Jesus,
you heard the cry of blind Bartimaeus
and restored his sight.
We pray for those whose lives are impaired
by handicap, disability and disadvantage,
especially . . .
Help us to defeat selfish prejudice
and bring your compassion
to the vulnerable and needy.
Jesus, Light of the World,
in your mercy, receive our prayer.

Lord Jesus,
you heard the last request of the penitent thief
as you hung on the Cross,
and promised him a place with you in Paradise.
We pray for all
whose lives are in confusion and disarray,
who feel unloved and unworthy
and do not know where to turn, especially . . .
Help us to accept those
whom others sideline and reject,
and reassure them of your unlimited love.
Jesus, Friend of Sinners,
in your mercy, receive our prayer.

Lord Jesus,
you wept with Mary and Martha
at the death of your friend Lazarus
and then restored him to life again.
We pray for all
who are enduring illness or infirmity,
anxiety or depression, loneliness or grief,
especially . . . who are known to us.
Help us to be faithful in prayer
and constant in care for them.
Jesus, the Resurrection and the Life,
in your mercy, receive our prayer.

Lord Jesus,
you often took time out
from your work of ministry
to spend time with your Father
in prayer and meditation.
We pray for our times of study and prayer
during this Lent,
especially . . .
Help us to resist the pressures and distractions
of our busy lives
and give time to deepening our faith.
Lord Jesus, Teacher and Guide,
in your mercy, receive our prayer.

Lord Jesus,
where two or three come together
in your name
you are present.
Hear and answer these prayers
in accordance with your will,
for your holy Name's sake.
Amen.

Our Father . . .

An alternative congregational response is the Taizé chant 'O Lord, hear my prayer' (HON 379) after each bidding.

Hymn

Father, hear the prayer we offer (HON 120)

Final prayer

**Lord,
when we are tempted
to put our trust in material things,
help us remember
that we live by the words of life
which come from you.
When we are tempted to put our trust
in religious rituals and practices,
help us remember
that love for you comes first.
When we are tempted
to seek power and acclaim,
help us remember that you alone
are worthy of worship and honour.
Amen.**

Blessing

May God the Father open our minds
to learn more of his grace.
Amen.

May God the Son open our hearts
to respond to his love.
Amen.

May God the Holy Spirit open our hands
to worship and serve him.
Amen.

And the blessing of God Almighty . . .

Choral music

Musically Lent is a time for restraint and thoughtfulness, not just because it is a season of penitence and prayer, but also to provide the greatest contrast with the joy and celebration of Easter Day. Allegri's 'Miserere', arguably the most famous of all settings of Psalm 51, perhaps makes excessive demands for an average church choir (and needs very fine soloists, too). Tallis' 'Lamentations of Jeremiah' also require much practice. However, there is plenty of prayerful music well within the compass of most choirs, not least the lovely compositions of Margaret Rizza, such as 'Silent, surrendered' or 'Fire of Love'. Any of her Contemplative Choral Music *pieces would grace a Lent ecumenical service as a devotional anthem. From* Anthems Old and New *could be selected Attwood's 'Turn thy face from my sins', Lloyd's arrangement of Stubbs' 'Not for our sins alone', Oxley's arrangement of Schein's 'O love, how deep' or Wesley's 'Wash me thoroughly', to mention just four.*

Alternative to the imposition of ashes

If there is a risk of confusion or division over imposing ashes, a similar act of penitence is to give each worshipper a small piece of paper and a pencil before the service starts. After the Liturgy of Penitence, a time of silence enables each person to write down some failing or personal issue that they want to bring to Christ. The congregation comes up as usual, and places the slips of paper into a fireproof container situated centrally on a table. The minister then lights a taper and sets fire to the pieces of paper, allowing them to burn until they are ash. The prayer before this needs slight variation from that above:

Prayer beforehand

We come to God in penitence and faith,
recognising his holiness and purity,
and conscious of our own unworthiness.
In penitence we bring before him now
the sins and failings we have written down
to be burned,
reminding us of our need to repent,
and reassuring us that they are forgiven
and completely forgotten.

Holy God,
we acknowledge in your sight
our wrongdoing and weaknesses,
written on these pieces of paper.
As we place them here
may we be reminded of how they have broken
our relationship with you,
and as they are burned
may we know they are blotted out for ever
by your love for us,
as we see it in your Son Jesus Christ,
who died that we might have eternal life.
Amen.

A REFLECTIVE SERVICE FOR LENT

Although more substantial services for the start of Lent and Palm Sunday are described in this book, it may be that church diaries make it impractical to organise something as elaborate as these. The reflective service described here is designed for use on the Fifth Sunday in Lent (Passion Sunday), but could be adapted for any of the others, or even used on a weekday. As with the reflective service for Advent, it can be led by anyone, ordained or lay, and is ideally suited to a smaller congregation.

Introduction

Jesus said: 'Anyone who loves his life will lose it, while anyone who hates his life in this world will keep it for eternal life. Whoever serves me must follow me, and where I am, my servant will also be.'

Silence

Song

Come and see (HON 88)

Prayer of approach

Lord Jesus,
Redeemer of the world,
you left your home in glory
to be lifted up on the earth
so that all people might be drawn to you.

As we look on you suffering humiliation,
and dying in agony on the cross,
may we also see you there
in power and majesty
In recognising you as victor
over sin and death,
may we know our sins forgiven,
and enter into eternal life with you.
Amen.

Responsive words of praise

Leader: Just as you have received Christ Jesus as Lord, continue to live in him; do not let your minds be captured by deceptive philosophies, which depend on human tradition and the principles of this world rather than on Christ.

Group A: In Christ the complete being of the Godhead lives in bodily form;
Group B: We have been brought to completion in him.

Group A: In Christ we have been purified by the removal of our sinful nature;
Group B: we have been buried with him in baptism, and raised with him through faith in the power of God.

Group A: In Christ God has made us alive by forgiving all our sins.
Group B: He took away the written law which condemns us, nailing it to the cross.

Group A: In Christ the powers and authorities of this world are disarmed.
Group B: He made a public spectacle of them, leading them as captives in his victory procession.

Leader: Since we have died with Christ to this world, let us therefore no longer behave as though we belonged to it, but set our hearts on things above.
(from Colossians 2)

First reading

Romans 8:6-11

Song

Lord Jesus Christ (HON 311)

Second reading

Mark 10:32-45

Meditation

The four evangelists are unanimous in portraying the disciples as decidedly human and fallible. Along with Simon Peter, James and John were the two disciples closest to Jesus, and not long before this disagreement they'd witnessed his transfiguration. Yet they still managed to get into an argument with the others over their future status in God's kingdom. Possibly they thought their closeness to their master entitled them to the place closest to him at the eternal banquet. Or maybe they simply thought their efforts deserved more recognition. It's interesting that Matthew records the involvement of James' and John's mother in the dispute. Whatever the motivation for their request, the effect was to trigger off a squabble with the other ten disciples, whose response was hardly more commendable – no doubt they all felt they should be granted the same special place!

Despite having seen and learned so much over the previous three years, the disciples hadn't yet understood that to share Jesus' status also involves sharing in his suffering, nor that in God's kingdom the values of this world are completely reversed. Following the way of Jesus doesn't mean we're automatically exempt from the temptation to seek status and power, and lord it over others. The divisions this causes have frequently torn the Church apart throughout its history. Too often we ask what we can do to project our image more effectively or gain more influence in the community, rather than asking what God wants us to do to serve those around. The only antidote is to turn the world's standards and values upside down as Jesus did, and choose instead the way of willing service, which will lead us through pain and inconvenience to true greatness.

Four questions to reflect on:

i. In what situations are we tempted to seek status or greater influence over others, and how can we resist this?

ii. How do we exercise authority and influence over others, and acknowledge those in authority over us?

iii. How willing are we to accept the role of servant for the sake of God's kingdom, and what might this involve?

iv. How willing are we to accept suffering or inconvenience as we follow Christ, and what might we find hardest to sacrifice?

Silent reflection

Passiontide response

We approach the throne of the Servant King,
who kneels and washes his disciples' feet,
saying, 'Lord Jesus, wash us clean';
make us alive in you.

When we feel tempted
to turn away from suffering
and choose the easy path,
Lord Jesus, wash us clean;
make us alive in you.

When we feel tempted
to seek personal recognition
and status above others,
Lord Jesus, wash us clean;
make us alive in you.

When we feel tempted
to pursue our own interests
but disregard the needs
of the underprivileged and exploited,
Lord Jesus, wash us clean;
make us alive in you.

When we feel tempted to strive for power
and forget our calling to serve others
in your name,
Lord Jesus, wash us clean;
make us alive in you.

As you have washed our feet,
setting us an example to follow,
may we do for others
what you have done for us,
for the sake of your kingdom. Amen.

Hymn

Praise to the Holiest in the height (HON 426)

Intercessions

We bring to God our prayers for all those who are faithfully serving him in hard or demanding situations, for all those whom we serve in our community, and for our shared commitment to Christ's way of humble service . . . *(a time of open intercession may follow, concluding with the Lord's Prayer).*

After each petition, or group of petitions, may be sung the Taizé chant 'Stay with me' (HON 458).

Song

From heaven you came (HON 148)

Final prayer

We ask God to put within us
the mind of Christ,
and make us willing to serve him
wherever he gives the opening.

In our homes and families
may we serve you joyfully.

At work and at leisure
may we serve you faithfully.

In times of stress and exertion
may we serve you loyally.

In times of quietness and reflection
may we serve you devotedly.

In times of sorrow and times of joy
**may we serve you wholeheartedly,
seeking no reward other than knowing
we are doing your will. Amen.**

Following the teaching of Jesus,
we pray as he taught:
Our Father . . .

For Jesus, who stoops in humility
to wash our feet,
let us bless the Lord.

For Jesus, the Servant King,
who gave his life to be a ransom for many,
thanks be to God.

MOTHERING SUNDAY OR A CELEBRATION OF THE FAMILY

Few Christian festivals can have undergone as many changes in recent years as Mothering Sunday. Its original emphasis on motherhood and 'mother church' eventually broadened into a celebration of Christian families, but family life today is quite different even from fifty years ago. Working mothers, single parents and restructured families are almost becoming the norm, while traditional patterns of family life have largely disintegrated under the weight of information technology, media influence and ease of travel. The Church has always championed the family as part of God's created order, but many people experience family life as anything but positive or joyful. Inevitably they feel uncomfortable or even offended if the liturgy rejoices in what they have found to be painful, or if it seems to exclude them because they cannot share the happy experiences of others. Any Christian celebration of the family, whether on Mothering Sunday or at some other time, must therefore be very sensitive to those who have suffered through family or marital breakdown, abusive treatment, inadequate parenting, or bereavement – and not least those who, to their great sadness, are unable to have children.

Outside LEPs Mothering Sunday may not be the easiest of Sundays on which to share worship with those of other traditions, though most would share the same concerns. An evening service may enable Churches to join together more easily, though this is likely to exclude younger children. Alternatively, it might be possible to organise a united service which focuses on the Christian concept of family without ignoring those who do not fit neatly into that framework, for whatever reason. This also provides an opportunity to emphasise the nurturing role of the local Church. The material in this outline service is based on Mothering Sunday, but could be used on any similar occasion and adapted to specific circumstances as required.

Opening response

We kneel in worship before our Father.
**Every family in heaven and on earth
takes its name from him.**

We pray that he will strengthen us
through his Spirit,
**that Christ may dwell in our hearts
through faith.**

We pray that we may be rooted
and established in love,
**that with all the saints
we may grasp the full extent of Christ's love.**

To the one who can do infinitely more
than we could ever imagine,
**to him be given glory
in the Church and in Jesus Christ
to every generation.**

Hymn

For the beauty of the earth (HON 137)

Prayer of thanksgiving

We give God thanks
for his gift of relationships and community,
saying, 'Lord, we give you thanks',
and praise your holy name.

For parental love and care,
which enfolds us in our early years,
Lord, we give you thanks,
and praise your holy name.

For a mother's love,
which nurtures and protects her children,
Lord, we give you thanks,
and praise your holy name.

For a father's care,
which supports and provides for his family,
Lord, we give you thanks,
and praise your holy name.

For the affection of brothers and sisters,
with whom childhood experiences are shared,
Lord, we give you thanks,
and praise your holy name.

For the support of wider family,
who share in joys and sorrows
and bring new horizons,

Lord, we give you thanks,
and praise your holy name.

For the loyalty and fellowship of friends,
who stay by us in good times and bad,
Lord, we give you thanks,
and praise your holy name.

For the Christian family,
with whom we share faith in Christ
and the hope of heaven,
Lord, we give you thanks,
**and praise your holy name,
the glory of Jesus Christ,
our Saviour and friend. Amen.**

Hymn

O Lord, all the world (HON 378)

Confession and absolution

Lord, we are sorry for the times
when we have failed to respect our parents
or encourage our families.
Lord, forgive our sin,
and help us to do your will.

We are sorry for the unkind words
and selfish actions
which spoil family life and love.
Lord, forgive our sin,
and help us to do your will.

We are sorry for the uncaring attitudes
and unfair judgements
which create unhappiness and resentment.
Lord, forgive our sin,
and help us to do your will.

We are sorry for the ingratitude
and self-centredness
which takes for granted
all that we have and enjoy.
Lord, forgive our sin,
**and help us to do your will,
to the honour and glory of your Son,
our Saviour Jesus Christ. Amen.**

Almighty God, merciful and forgiving Father,
pardon all our sin, in thought, word and deed,
and restore us to a right relationship
with you and with one another,
through Jesus Christ our Lord. Amen.

Song

Lord, we come to ask your healing (HON 319)

First reading

Exodus 2:1-10 or
1 Samuel 1:20-28

Anthem

'Father of all' (Tambling)
Anthems Old and New

Second reading

Colossians 3:12-17 or
Luke 2:39-52

Hymn

For Mary, mother of our Lord (HON 136) or
Jesus put this song into our hearts (HON 275)

Address

Response

To enable the congregation to express their common membership of God's family, invite them in advance to bring to the service a symbol of the practical care they show to someone else, or would be willing to show. For children, a bottle of washing-up liquid or shoe-cleaning wax would illustrate ways they could show care for a parent or older person – the sort of task for which badges are awarded by uniformed organisations such as Cubs and Brownies. However, adults should not be let off the hook! DIY tools and aids, gardening implements, kitchen utensils or an iron come readily to mind as symbols of practical ways of showing Christian care. For those not blessed with practical skills, care might mean help with finances, transport, childminding, dog walking, sitting with an elderly person for a couple of hours to relieve a carer, or getting involved with local concerns such as road safety – a bit of creative thought will soon identify an appropriate symbol for any of these. Everyone who brings something should be invited at this point to bring them up to a focal point (ideally, though not necessarily, an altar or communion table).

Intercession

We bring to God our prayers
and concerns for families;

for those who find family life
to be a source of unhappiness and tension,
and for those who have no family.
Lord of love,
receive this prayer.

For families on the verge of breakdown,
unsure where to find relief
or a way out of their difficulties . . .
May they know your guidance and wisdom
to find an outcome
which brings peace to their hearts.
Lord of love,
receive this prayer.

For children who are frightened and insecure,
neglected or abused
by those they trust and rely on . . .
May they know your loving hand
on their lives,
and find in you a friend who is always faithful.
Lord of love,
receive this prayer.

For those whose family life is overshadowed
by addiction or violence,
who live with the consequences of alcohol
or drug abuse . . .
May they know your peace
and encouragement
in helping those unable to help themselves.
Lord of love,
receive this prayer.

For families without a home
or adequate resources,
whose life is a struggle for survival . . .
May they know the hope you alone can give,
and trust you to bring them
through their troubles.
Lord of love,
receive this prayer.

For those without family or friends,
who experience the pain of loneliness
as a result of bereavement, divorce
or the absence of friendship . . .
May they know your eternal presence
alongside,
reassuring and comforting them.

Lord of love,
receive this prayer,
which we ask in the name of your Son,
Jesus Christ our Lord. Amen.

Our Father . . .

Song

A new commandment (HON 4) or
Let there be love (HON 298)

Final prayer

Lord, bless the homes we now go to;
make them open and welcoming
in your name.

Lord, bless the families we now return to;
make them signs of your love and care.

Lord, bless the lives we now continue with;
make them worthy of your kingdom.

Lord, bless and guide us,
whatever we do, wherever we go.
Go before us, watch over us
and keep us in your love,
for the sake of Jesus Christ, our Lord. Amen.

Hymn

Bind us together (HON 60) or
Now thank we all our God (HON 354)

Blessing

PALM SUNDAY

Coming both at the end of the forty days of
Lent and the start of Holy Week, Palm Sunday
encompasses penitence and the passion of our
Lord as well as the immediately obvious
element of celebration and rejoicing. In most
places it will also mark the end of Lent study
groups and the beginning of the drama of
Holy Week. Palm crosses and processions
spring readily to mind, and are accepted by
most mainstream denominations, forming a
welcome part of our own LEP's observation
of Holy Week. However, a large-scale event

involving several Churches is probably best
arranged for an evening. Our own Churches
Together group has for some years used this as
a way of drawing the Lent studies to a conclusion, and at the same time allowing some of
the practical fruits of these to be used in the
worship. Music groups, drama groups, flower
arrangers, painters and writers have all made
their contribution to the service. It is worth
pointing out that to do this successfully requires a church building which can be adapted
to such a variety of uses. In the following service outline, hymns, readings and prayers are
suggested, to fit in with this pattern.

Introductory sentence

In this is love, not that we loved God but that
he loved us, and sent his Son to be the atoning
sacrifice for our sins (1 John 4:10).

Opening response

We do not preach the Gospel with words of
human wisdom, lest the cross of Christ be
emptied of its power. The message of the cross
makes no sense to those who are perishing,
but to us who are being saved
it is the power of God.

God has made foolish the cleverness of the
scholar and philosopher,
for the world cannot know God
through wisdom.

Through the folly of what is preached,
God is pleased to save those who believe.

The foolishness of God is infinitely wiser than
human wisdom;
his wisdom is infinitely greater
than human strength.

Hymn

Ride on, ride on in majesty (HON 435)

Confession and absolution

At the start of Holy Week we come to the cross
of Christ in sorrow and penitence for the sins
which he bore there.

Lord Jesus,
we turn to you in faith,
repenting of our wrongdoing
and seeking your pardon.
Merciful Lord, forgive and heal us.

We have acted in our own strength,
and not put our trust wholly in you.
Merciful Lord, forgive and heal us.

We have been arrogant and proud,
and not humbled ourselves before you.
Merciful Lord, forgive and heal us.

We have acted out of self-interest,
and not shown your love or compassion
to those in need.
Merciful Lord, forgive and heal us.

We have lived as though you had no part
in our lives,
and not acknowledged you as Lord.
**Merciful Lord, forgive and heal us.
Turn our failings into strengths,
and our weaknesses into opportunities
for the sake of your kingdom. Amen.**

May the God of forgiveness
show you his mercy,
forgive your sins, and bring you to eternal life,
through Jesus Christ our Lord. Amen.

Hymn

My song is love unknown (HON 346)

Prayer at close of study groups

God our Father,
at the close of our time of reflection and study
we thank you for new insights into your love,
new bonds of fellowship forged,
and renewed strength to continue walking
in the way of Christ.
Make us stronger in faith,
draw us closer to you and each other,
and deepen our knowledge and experience
of your love and grace
as we see it revealed
in the death of our Saviour on the cross,
in whose name we pray. Amen.

First reading

Isaiah 50:4-9a

Introduction to presentations

This should be as brief as possible, and those responsible for each group should be aware of the time limits imposed. It may be helpful to give some background information for the benefit of those who have not taken part in any groups, not least on how they relate to the theme of the Lent studies. It should also be clear how they fit in with the rest of the liturgy. Three examples only are given here, though more can be added as appropriate. However, time will be limited; the more time given to presentations, the less will be available for other elements of the liturgy – and don't forget to take into account the hidden time lost between each item, which can increase greatly without anyone noticing!

Drama group

Song

My Lord, what love is this? (HON 345)

Second reading

Matthew 21:1-13

Music group

Song

You are the King of Glory (HON 570)

Third reading

Philippians 2:1-11

Dance group

Song

Brother, sister, let me serve you (HON 73)

Meditation

Intercessions

We bring our prayers to Jesus,
despised and rejected,
saying, Lord of love,
hear our cry.

Lord Jesus,
criticised, mocked and condemned as a criminal,
we pray for all who suffer ill-treatment
or ridicule for their faith,
especially . . .
May they stand firm in their faith
and remain joyful in their faith.
Lord of love,
hear our cry.

Lord Jesus,
arrested wrongly and tried unfairly,
we pray for all who suffer
as a result of injustice and oppression,
especially . . .
May they be given courage and patience
to be true to themselves and you.
Lord of love,
hear our cry.

Lord Jesus,
jeered at by crowds and flogged by soldiers,
we pray for all
who suffer physical or mental abuse,
especially . . .
May they receive comfort and assurance
in their troubles
and relief from persecution.
Lord of love,
hear our cry.

Lord Jesus,
nailed to the cross in cruel pain,
we pray for all who suffer in mind or body,
especially . . .
May they receive healing and peace from you,
the wounded healer.
Lord of love,
hear our cry.

Lord Jesus,
utterly alone as you died,
we pray for all who suffer isolation
or the loneliness of grief,
especially . . .
May they find in you the faithful friend
who will never let them down.
Lord of love,
hear our cry
and bring to our lives
the wonder of your healing
and the joy of your salvation,
to the glory of your name. Amen.

Hymn

I, the Lord of sea and sky (HON 235)

Prayer for Holy Week

Lord,
the paradoxes of your passion and death
bewilder us:
the King of Glory is crucified
with common thieves;
the one who knew no sin
takes our sins upon himself;
the Lord of life dies in agony;
the scene of humiliating defeat
becomes the place of final victory
over sin and death.
By your life may we live for you;
by your death may we die to sin;
by your resurrection may we rise
to eternal life
for your holy name's sake. Amen.

Final response

As we run the race set before us,
keep us firm in faith and steadfast in hope.

As we continue our earthly pilgrimage,
keep our eyes fixed on Jesus.

As we look for the coming of your kingdom,
we pray together,
Our Father . . .

Blessing and dismissal

GOOD FRIDAY

Among the most popular ecumenical activities of the last decade has been the Good Friday procession or 'walk of witness', which takes place in many towns during the morning, often to enable those Churches which do so to keep their three-hour vigil, starting at 12 noon. In a busy shopping area this can be a powerful witness to the secular world, but many Christians are unable to participate because they have to work themselves. In any event, in many locations a procession would be impractical or have little impact. In the more Catholic tradition, the three-hour vigil would be kept, but this is now often reduced to 'the last hour', a devotional reflection on the cross.

Our LEP has adopted an ecumenical approach to the three-hour vigil, and, while it needs a bit of fine-tuning, both traditions have found it helpful. Broadly, the first hour is devotional and reflective; the second is unstructured, but with visual material at various points in the worship area, which can be used for personal meditation on the passion; the third is more liturgical. A children's workshop runs in parallel with the first two hours, enabling parents to take part in the liturgy if they wish, but also, in the second hour, enabling the ministers to spend some time with the children, and lead them in a short time of worship. The final hour enables the children's leaders to share in formal worship as well. However, there is no reason why two churches fairly close to each other should not work out a similar pattern. The following outline shows one way of handling the first and third hours, but that should not detract from the importance of the time spent with the children – it is quite feasible to link their themes with those the adults have been considering.

The First Hour
Opening response

Jesus himself bore our sins in his body
on the tree,
so that we might die to sin
and live for righteousness.
By his wounds we have been healed.

The punishment that brought us peace
was upon him.
By his wounds we have been healed.

Hymn
There is a green hill (HON 499)

Prayer

Glory be to you, Almighty Father,
for your limitless and pervasive love
with which we are confronted on the cross.

We feel ashamed and unworthy
to stand in your presence,
and acknowledge our failure to respond
to your gracious act of sending your Son
to bring us back to you.
Lord, have mercy.
Lord, have mercy.

Glory be to you, Lord Jesus, Son of God,
humiliated and crucified King of kings,
for your perfect obedience in going to the cross
to win us freedom from sin and death.
We feel sorrowful and contrite
at the sins which nailed you there,
and ask you to forgive and restore us
to the path which leads to eternal life.
Christ, have mercy,
Christ, have mercy.

Glory be to you, Holy Spirit of God,
for your persistent troubling of our conscience,
and your reassurance that on the cross
love has conquered the power of evil and death.
We feel joyful that your grace
has won our forgiveness,
and praise you for the hope
which is set before us.
Lord, have mercy,
Lord, have mercy.

Through the cross of Christ
may God have mercy on us,
pardon us, and set us free,
that we might be strengthened in faith
and kept in eternal life. Amen.

Lord Jesus,
remember us in your kingdom as we pray:
Our Father . . .

Hymn
My song is love unknown (HON 346)

Readings
Lamentations 5:15-22
John 19:17-30

Hymn
Come and see (HON 88)

Reflection/Meditation

As we read the accounts of Jesus' arrest, trial, crucifixion and burial, we see a cast of characters watching, participating and reacting to the events leading up to the cross. In viewing them we see ourselves reflected: our words which aren't translated into action; our refusal to acknowledge Jesus through fear of other people; our determination to prove we're right; our vain attempts to sit on the fence.

There's Peter, sitting by the fire, trying to keep warm – and keep his head down. Full of fine words when things are going well, he's already got into trouble by injuring a servant's ear, so now he's playing safe and keeping it all at arm's length. His protestations that he'll never deny his master are soon to be tested and found wanting. Not that we'd ever do such a thing . . . But too often we try to keep out of trouble, and make sure we're not really associated with Jesus. It's easy to say all the right words in church, but the acid test comes when we engage with the world for the rest of the week. The soft option is to pretend we're being reasonable, and open to all views. The tough option is openly to follow the way of Jesus, the suffering servant.

Then there's Nicodemus, the religious leader who came to Jesus by night so no one would see him and tell the tabloids. He knew in his heart that Jesus was someone special, whose words rang true, whose life matched them. He recognised, however dimly, the words and work of God in this wandering rabbi. Yet only after Jesus' death does he take any risk by offering to help with Jesus' burial. So much of our behaviour is conditioned by our fear of other people, their reactions, their scorn, their rejection, their condemnation. If we are to follow the way of Jesus, we can't keep our heads below the parapet in case someone disapproves. Our response to his love means potentially accepting the sneering, the abuse and the rejection which he endured.

On the other hand we can look at Caiaphas and his fellow priests, all totally convinced that they're doing the right thing and preserving the true religion of Israel. It never occurs to them that their actions run counter to all that God is and does. We condemn the grossly unfair trial and unjust sentence, yet have to recognise the pride and arrogance within us which is determined to be proved right at all costs, even if others have to suffer. In complete contrast, Jesus never condemns, but looks with sorrow on the whole system in Jerusalem which rejects his Father's love in the belief that it alone is right.

Finally, what of Pilate, whose ritual ablutions have never exonerated him for his part in Jesus' death? He thought he could stand aside from it and push the responsibility elsewhere, but his refusal to make a decision didn't remove his name from the narrative. Jesus just won't let us sit on the fence and be objective, because he's not a Greek philosopher but our Saviour.

The characters of the Good Friday story make us face our own response to the cross: the pain and agony of the dying Jesus; the jeering of the crowds; the fear of the authorities; the apparent defeat of all that is good and pure and holy. Yet, if we want to share in the victory of the cross, we must share too in its suffering. In responding to the love poured out on that civic rubbish tip, where three Roman gibbets were hastily erected, we rule out arrogance, pride, cowardice and apathy.

Hymn

Were you there when they crucified my Lord?
(HON 540)

Intercessions

As our Saviour lays down his life for us on the cross, we bring to him our thanksgiving and requests, saying,
Lord of love, hear our prayer;
let our cry come to you.

Lord Jesus,
on the cross you were willing to forgive
those who mocked and jeered at you.
We pray for those who refuse
to recognise you as king or own you as Lord,
who despise what is good
and rejoice in the unworthy, especially . . .
May their eyes be opened
to see your dying love,
and their hearts to respond
to its transforming power.
Lord of love, hear our prayer;
let our cry come to you.

Lord Jesus,
on the cross you asked the disciple you loved
to care for your mother.
We pray for those whose grief or loneliness
make them feel vulnerable and disadvantaged,
especially . . .
May they know the strength and comfort
of your eternal presence
through the care and compassion
of the Christian community.
Lord of love, hear our prayer;
let our cry come to you.

Lord Jesus,
on the cross you forgave a common criminal
crucified with you,
and offered him a place in your kingdom.
We pray for those
who feel unworthy and rejected,
who are left on the margins of society,
especially . . .
May they know your acceptance and welcome
through the ministry of your people.
Lord of love, hear our prayer;
let our cry come to you.

Lord Jesus,
on the cross a Roman centurion recognised
what others failed to see
and praised God.
We pray for those whose faith is growing,
who are at a key point
in their spiritual journey,
especially . . .
May they move onwards in the Christian life
as they learn more of your love
and enter more fully into your risen life.
Lord of love, hear our prayer;
let our cry come to you.

Lord Jesus,
on the cross you were obedient to your Father
in facing death to win for us eternal life.
May we be strengthened
to follow your example
of selfless love and service.
Lord of love, hear our prayer;
**let our cry come to you.
As your love dwells in us
so may we love one another**

for the sake of Jesus Christ,
our crucified Lord. Amen.

Hymn

When I survey the wondrous cross (HON 549)

Closing response

Lord of the joyful procession,
may we worship you wholeheartedly.

Lord of the upper room,
may we dine with you for ever.

Lord of the desolate garden,
may we watch and wait with you.

Lord of the unjust sentence,
may we pursue justice and peace.

Lord of the cruel cross,
may we be willing to suffer with you.

Lord of the empty tomb,
may we rise with you to eternal life.

Blessing

The Second Hour

The minister(s) now go to where the children are working on material connected with the Good Friday theme. Meanwhile the worshippers are free to stand or sit by the various displays and meditate on the significance of what they have seen and heard. We mix traditional visual symbols, such as icons, a purple robe, a copy of a painting of the crucifixion, with modern images, such as a collage of suffering built up from press pictures. Appropriate quiet music is played in the background. Each year the children have a different approach. One particularly effective idea was to take the fourteen Stations of the Cross and produce a 'news report' on each of them, to pull together into a 'documentary' of the events of the first Good Friday. The act of worship is very informal, but aims to help the children make sense of what they have been doing in the wider context of the day. Kidsource has some excellent songs for this kind of children's event: 'There on a cruel cross' (328), 'I will offer up my life' (186), 'Jesus, thank you for the cross' (214), 'I'm special' (162) and 'God never gives up' (83) are particularly suitable.

The Final Hour

Silence

Opening prayer

Lord Jesus Christ,
on the cross at Calvary
your hands were ripped by cruel nails,
hands that stretched out
to offer healing, comfort and acceptance.
Make our hands open
to the pain that comes from serving you,
open to reach out with your love
to the broken and needy.
Lord, we offer you our hands.

Lord Jesus Christ,
as you hung on the cross
your feet were pierced,
feet that approached the despised,
and walked alongside those
condemned as sinners.
Make our feet willing to go where you lead us,
unafraid of sneering or rejection.
Lord, we offer you our feet.

Lord Jesus Christ,
on the cross your side was torn open
with a soldier's spear,
your body freely given up
for love of those who did not love you.
Make us strong to withstand opposition
and ridicule,
knowing your love overcomes
the power of evil.
Lord, we offer you our bodies.

Lord Jesus Christ,
as you died in agony on the cross
your heart was broken
by the rebellion and rejection
of your own people,
by our sin which nailed you there.
Make our hearts clean and pure,
dedicated to your service
and filled with your love.
**Lord, we offer you our hearts and lives
to be a living sacrifice.**

Old Testament reading

Isaiah 52:12-53:12

Hymn

My Lord, what love is this (HON 345)

New Testament reading

Hebrews 4:14-16, 5:7-9

Hymn

Meekness and majesty (HON 335)

Gospel reading

Luke 23:13-49

Meditation

In the first hour of the vigil the meditation looked at how some of the characters in the passion narrative responded to the events leading up to Jesus' crucifixion. Here we see how some of them respond to Jesus himself, as he hangs in agony on the cross.

One character who plays a large part in all the Gospel accounts is Pontius Pilate. He tries hard to pretend it's 'not my problem', but even his unwillingness to make a decision has its consequences. He knows the decision to release Barabbas, a political terrorist, is totally against all principles of justice, Jewish or Roman, but for a quiet life he lets it through. John records that the authorities wanted the inscription above Jesus' head to be changed, to say 'this man claimed to be the King of the Jews', but Pilate now refuses to budge. His response to Jesus is by no means one of opposition, but rather of ambiguity. Perhaps deep down he recognises that here is a man of such authority as he's never before encountered.

Luke alone tells of the 'penitent thief', a common criminal crucified by chance alongside Jesus, who condemns his friend for joining in the laughter and insults against Jesus. His comment indicates that he too is aware, however dimly, that he is in the presence of true kingship. His response is hardly dramatic, while his final request contains no expectation of forgiveness or pardon. Yet Jesus at once offers him a place in his kingdom; even the act of recognising who Jesus really is opens up a chink through which God's love and grace can come flooding through. The other criminal is unmoved, and, though quite unaware of it, the abusive and sarcastic crowd of onlookers stand just as much under condemnation as he does.

Typically, Luke also highlights two foreigners. Simon of Cyrene was perhaps just a large, strong man who happened to be nearby when the cross needed to be carried. We know little about him, but he seems to have carried out his duty without complaint, though as a member of an ethnic minority he may well have felt exploited. And after Jesus' death a Roman centurion, equally despised by true Jews, shows far greater understanding of the identity and mission of this extraordinary victim of a gross miscarriage of justice than do his fellow countrymen. No wonder Jesus wept when he saw Jerusalem.

None of these characters would have fitted in with the Jewish authorities – only one of them was a Jew, and he was from the bottom of the social pile. Yet, as Luke shows us, their part in the events was significant enough to warrant being written down. It's easy to write people off because they don't quite 'belong', or conform to the norms of a particular group. But if we're to follow the way of Jesus, we have to welcome and accept those who may well have been written off or rejected by others. And while it may gall those who've been going to church most of their lives, God's love needs only the tiniest gap in our self-defence system through which to start pouring in. As the penitent thief found out, no one can do anything to win a place in heaven. In that briefest of conversations with Jesus, he discovered that God's grace can overcome and transform even the murkiest past and the darkest character.

Hymn
O sacred head surrounded (HON 389)

Good Friday Litany
(during which a simple wooden cross can be brought to a central position)

Lord of the cross of shame
we feel your pain.

Lord,
in the desolation of this earth
through our greed and exploitation,
we feel your pain.

Lord,
in the refugee camps and shanty towns
we feel your pain.
Lord,
in the streets which are home
to unloved and unwanted children
we feel your pain.
Lord,
in the courts which hear only the voice
of the rich and powerful
we feel your pain.
Lord,
in the prison cells and torture chambers
we feel your pain.
Lord,
in the killing fields,
heavy with death and despair
we feel your pain.
Lord,
in the barricaded streets and riot-torn cities
we feel your pain.
Lord,
in the cry of the abused child,
in the sigh of the lonely elderly
we feel your pain.

Lord of the cross of forgiveness,
have mercy on us.
We have been greedy and selfish;
have mercy on us.
We have shut our eyes to need and poverty;
have mercy on us.
We have been unkind and uncaring;
have mercy on us.
We have been unfair in our judgements;
have mercy on us.
We have not acted as peacemakers
and bridge-builders,
have mercy on us.
We have turned away from the cry of pain
and the plea for help;
have mercy on us.

Lord of the cross of glory,
we share in your victory.

In times of injustice
we show your compassion.
In times of hatred
we show your love.
In times of fear
we bring your peace.
In times of conflict
we bring your reconciling grace.
In times of despair
we bring your joy.
In times of uncertainty and suspicion
we bring your truth.

Hymn

We sing the praise of him who died
(HON 536)

Intercessions

We lay at the foot of the cross the prayers
which lie on our hearts:
For the unity of Christ's Church
throughout the world,
for the removal of all barriers
which prevent closer fellowship
in the Christian faith . . .
Hear us, O Lord,
accept our prayer.

For the united witness and service
of all God's people,
for our shared mission and outreach
to our own community and area . . .
Hear us, O Lord,
accept our prayer.

For the leaders of the world,
and especially our own nation,
for greater commitment everywhere
to following the ways of justice
and righteousness . . .
Hear us, O Lord,
accept our prayer.

For members of other faith communities,
for the removal of all bigotry
and resentment
which would preclude
greater mutual understanding . . .
Hear us, O Lord,
accept our prayer.

For those who have not heard or responded
to the good news of Jesus Christ,
those who reject it,
those who ill-treat Christians,
those whose faith has been swamped
by the suffering and turmoil of this life . . .
Hear us, O Lord,
accept our prayer.

For those who suffer in body, mind or spirit,
for the chronically and terminally ill,
the depressed and anxious,
the lonely and grieving,
the abused and neglected . . .
Hear us, O Lord,
accept our prayer.

For aid-workers and educators,
for carers and counsellors,
and for all who in Christ's name
bring help to the suffering
and relief to the needy . . .
Hear us, O Lord,
accept our prayer.

For ourselves,
that we may display the unity which is ours
through the death of our Lord Jesus Christ,
in joyful worship, loving fellowship
and compassionate service . . .
Hear us, O Lord,
accept our prayer,
and bring us
with all who have died in the faith of Christ
to the joy of eternal life,
through Christ our Lord. Amen.

Our Father . . .

Final prayer

God our Father,
you sent your Son Jesus Christ to the cross,
that through his death and resurrection
we might know forgiveness of our sins,
the joy of salvation
and the hope of eternal life.
Transformed by his love
may we die to sin and live to righteousness,
and share in his victory over death and evil.
Amen.

EASTER, ASCENSION AND PENTECOST

The greatest change of mood in the Christian Year comes as the excitement and celebration of Easter bursts in on the darkness of the preceding days and weeks. The Early Church was quite clear that Easter was the Church's most important festival, and despite the best efforts of the retail trade and others, the hype and frenzy of Christmas has not altered this in any of the mainstream churches. The programme for Easter Day itself is therefore likely to be well fixed in every church diary, so other than in full-blown LEPs this may not be the most convenient day to organise an ecumenical service. However, there may be scope for using one of the Sundays of Eastertide to join together in an Easter Praise service.

Where Lent as a season is best suited to a more structured and reflective approach to worship, Easter lends itself to spontaneity and joyful praise. The last three decades have seen a great increase in the number of churches incorporating a 'praise service' into their programme, often on a Sunday evening. While the initial impetus for this came from the Charismatic Renewal, other factors have kept it going: the inclusion of newer worship songs, the need to use a worship group, and, not least, the desire to let the breeze of God's Holy Spirit blow away some of the long-established dust and cobwebs of more formal liturgy! The television programme *Songs of Praise* has also proved enduringly popular, and established a format for worship which has appealed even to Churches where there are reservations about adopting unstructured praise services. As a result, there are plenty of 'Praise and Prayer', 'Celebration Praise' and 'Songs of Praise' services which owe little to the traditional worshipping practices of the mainstream Churches, but provide a common approach for most of them. This may not go down too well among liturgical purists, but it provides a simple and widely accepted style for ecumenical worship.

However, simplicity is often more difficult to achieve than might appear on the surface. There may be less formality, but some kind of structure is essential if the service is to be meaningful to all present and draw them together into worshipping the risen Lord. An overdose of unfamiliar, brand-new worship songs, excessive use of someone's in-house jargon, or plain uncertainty about what is going to happen next, all create a sense of unease in any congregation, not least one drawn from several different traditions. Spontaneity is especially tricky to handle. It requires a delicate balance between allowing people to express their worship in a personal, informal way, without this either degenerating into liturgical anarchy, or becoming the exclusive preserve of those who are familiar with it, to the exclusion of everyone else. Times of 'open worship' therefore need to be balanced with more set patterns that enable everyone to participate. Music can also become an issue in these less structured services. They offer an excellent opportunity to learn some of the very good new hymns and worship songs now available, but these need to be practised and taught in a way that enables everyone to sing, and balanced with better-known items. Most important of all, an act of worship needs a sense of direction and purpose if those taking part in it are to feel they have been inspired and challenged.

The following service outlines are for Easter, Ascensiontide and Pentecost, and are based on three different 'Praise Service' formats: one is loosely constructed on the pattern of Evening Prayer, the second follows television's *Songs of Praise*, and the third is a somewhat freer 'Praise and Prayer' pattern. More than in other liturgical forms, the suggested material can be replaced by open, extempore words of praise and prayer, but it is worth retaining some elements which can be shared by all. Please remember, it can be very tempting to describe an unstructured sequence of songs, prayers and shared thoughts as 'a time of worship' – it is, but so is the rest of the service!

EASTER EVENING PRAISE

Opening response

We meet together in the presence
of the living God;
we have come to worship him.
With angels, and the whole company
of heaven,
we have come to worship him.
With rivers and mountains, stars and planets,
and the whole of creation.
we have come to worship him.

We meet together in the presence
of the risen Christ;
we have come to exalt him.
With the apostles and saints,
we have come to exalt him.
With the Church in every age
and Christians in every nation,
we have come to exalt him.

We meet together in the presence
of the life-giving Spirit;
we have come to praise him.
With psalms, hymns and spiritual songs,
we have come to praise him.
With joy and gladness in our hearts,
we have come to praise him.

Hymn

Jesus is Lord (HON 270)

Confession and absolution

Living Lord,
raised from death, victorious over evil,
we confess to you our sins and wrongdoing.
By your mighty power,
raise us with you to eternal life.

Living Lord,
by your death and resurrection
you have destroyed the clutches of sin.
Forgive us when we yield to temptation,
and by your mighty power,
raise us with you to eternal life.

Living Lord,
by your death and resurrection
you have won for us freedom and new life.
Forgive us when we allow guilt and fear
to dominate our lives,
and by your mighty power,
raise us with you to eternal life.

Living Lord,
by your death and resurrection
you have opened the way to eternal life.
Forgive us when we live without thinking
about our home in heaven,
and by your mighty power,
**raise us with you to eternal life
and set our minds
on the things which are above,
where you reign for ever. Amen.**

Almighty God,
who raised our Lord Jesus from the dead,
forgive all you have done wrong,
and raise you from the death of sin
to the life of righteousness,
through Jesus Christ our Lord. Amen.

Alternative confession

Praise the Lord, O my soul,
and do not forget his benefits.
Lord, have mercy;
Lord, have mercy.

He forgives all my sins
and heals all my diseases.
Christ, have mercy;
Christ, have mercy.

He redeems my life from the pit,
and crowns me with love and compassion.
Lord, have mercy;
Lord, have mercy.

Song

We will lay our burden down (HON 538)

First reading

Isaiah 65:17-25 or
Acts 10:34-43 or
1 Corinthians 15:1-11 or
1 Peter 2:19-25

Songs and hymns

Chosen from:
All heaven declares (HON 14)
Alleluia, Alleluia, give thanks to the risen Lord
(HON 24)
Led like a lamb (HON 294)
Jesus, Jesus, holy and anointed one (HON 271)
We believe (Source 541)
For this purpose (Source 111)

Second reading

Matthew 27:62-28:10 or
Luke 24:13-35 or
John 20:19-29 or
John 21:1-14

Songs and hymns

Chosen from:
In the tomb so cold (Source 234)
He is Lord (HON 204)
He has risen (Source 155)
Be still, for the presence of the Lord (HON 53)
Jesus, we celebrate your victory (Source 299)

Time of shared reflections and insights

In the context of ecumenical worship it can be very stimulating to hear the fruits and insights of others' meditations. However, opening this to the congregation runs the risk that one or two folk with bees buzzing in their bonnets will seize the opportunity to hold forth at length. To try and avoid this, you could invite a couple of people in advance to share their thoughts for a minute or so, thus setting a pattern for others. Alternatively, you could either suggest specific subjects for contributions, or invite people to group in threes or fours to exchange their ideas, though this may be restricted or precluded both by the building and the numbers present. Whichever you prefer, it would be wise to indicate a clear time limit at the outset.

Hymn

I, the Lord of sea and sky (HON 235)

Time of open thanksgiving and intercession

Response after each section

Risen Master,
receive our prayer.

Alternatively use the Taizé song 'The Lord is my song' (HON 487) as a response.

Our Father . . .

Final prayer

For the power which rolled away the stone
from the tomb,
Risen Master,
receive our praise.

For the love which called Mary by name
in the garden,
Risen Master,
receive our praise.

For the joy which energised the disciples
to run and tell their friends the good news,
Risen Master,
receive our praise.

For the strength which helps us day by day
to walk by faith,
Risen Master,
receive our praise.

For the hope which reassures us of eternal life,
starting now,
Risen Master,
receive our praise.
Transform us by your risen power,
restore us with your undying love,
and strengthen us by your Spirit ever with us,
through Jesus Christ our Lord. Amen.

Closing hymn

Thine be the glory (HON 503)

Blessing

May God the Father,
who raised our Saviour Jesus Christ
from death,
give us freedom from sin and death,
to live by faith instead of fear.
Amen.

May Christ, the Son of God,
who was obedient even to death on a cross,
give us freedom and hope,
to live in the light of eternal life.
Amen.

May the Holy Spirit of God,
who guides us into all truth,
give us strength to live for God
day by day.
Amen.

ASCENSIONTIDE

Ascension Day invariably falls on a Thursday, at the end of the 'great forty days', but while this provides a fitting culmination to the Easter celebrations, it tends to fall a bit flat liturgically by coming in the middle of the working week. From an ecumenical viewpoint, the non-conformist Churches in general tend to make less of it than Anglicans and Roman Catholics, for both of whom worship would normally be eucharistic, but the inevitably lower midweek attendance might be offset by extending an invitation more widely to other traditions. However, a service on the seventh Sunday of Easter is likely to be a more practical ecumenical option, so this outline uses the *Songs of Praise* format.

This is a time in the Christian year when hymns and songs for a wide range of seasons and themes are suitable, which gives plenty of scope to those invited to choose one. Experience suggests that hymns of praise and rejoicing are among the most popular, followed by those in a more devotional style. Ideally the choices should be explained by those who've made them, which can be done very effectively (and more briefly!) by using an interviewer to elicit information.

While an informal feel is a great asset to this kind of service, a basic structure is necessary to hold it all together, and the spontaneity of the contributions is ideally offset by slightly more formal elements. Prayer which everyone present can join in will both draw worshippers together and provide a fixed point to which everyone can relate, and a Bible reading also gives the necessary common focus. The interviews/explanations preclude the need for any other spoken input, but they should be separated into blocks of two or at most three so that the overall impact is not that of a lengthy

sermon! Musical resources may restrict the choice of hymns – modern worship songs with a syncopated blues or jazz rhythm can sound distinctly odd on an organ, while *Jerusalem* would require a virtuoso worship group! Clearly those invited to participate should be given as free a choice of hymns or songs as possible, but the suggestions below might serve as a guideline.

Opening response

We have a great high priest
who has passed through the heavens,
Jesus, the Son of God.
**You are worthy, O Lord our God,
to receive glory, honour and power.**

God raised him from the dead
and seated him at his right hand
in the heavenly realms.
**You are worthy, O Lord our God,
to receive glory, honour and power.**

Therefore God exalted him to the highest place
and gave him the name above all other names,
that at the name of Jesus every knee should bow.
**You are worthy, O Lord our God,
to receive glory, honour and power.**

Hymn

At the name of Jesus (HON 46)

Confession

Lord Jesus Christ, King of Glory,
you left your home in heaven
to share our earthly life
and die for us on the cross.
We are sorry we have not loved you
with all our heart.
In your mercy,
forgive and help us.

You rose from the grave
as victor over sin and death.
We are sorry we have not lived
in the light of eternal life.
In your mercy,
forgive and help us.

You ascended into heaven,
where you reign for ever with the Father.
We are sorry we have not always
acknowledged you as our king.
In your mercy,
forgive and help us.
Make us joyful in worship
and obedient in service,
to the praise and glory of your name. Amen.

Absolution

Almighty God,
Father of our Lord Jesus Christ,
pardon and deliver you from all your sin,
that you may live in the light of his presence,
walk with him by faith
and reign with him in glory,
through Jesus Christ our Lord. Amen.

Interviews/testimonies

Hymns or songs

Chosen from:
He is exalted (HON 203)
Majesty (HON 327)
Rejoice, the Lord is King (HON 432)
The head that once was crowned with thorns
(HON 480)

Reading

Acts 1:1-11 or
Ephesians 1:15-23

Prayer

We ask you, Lord God,
Father of our Lord Jesus Christ,
for the gift of your Spirit,
to reveal him to us,
that we might know him better;
to open our eyes,
that we might see his light
and know the hope we are called to;
to open our hearts,
that we might receive the riches
of his grace and power,
available to all who believe,
through Jesus Christ our Lord. Amen.

Interviews/testimonies

Hymns or songs

Chosen from:
Hail the day that sees him rise (HON 191)
Jesus shall take the highest honour (HON 278)
The Lord is King! (HON 485)
You are the King of Glory (HON 570)

Reading

Matthew 28:16-20 or
Luke 24:44-53

Prayer

Lord Jesus,
to you has been given all authority
in heaven and on earth.
Yours is the name above every other name,
the name to which the greatest
and the least will bow.
In your name
may we go out together from here
to obey the great commission
which you give to all who follow you:
to make disciples among all the peoples
of the world,
to baptise them in the name of the Trinity,
and to teach them to obey
your commands and will.
And in going out
may we know the reality of your promise
to be with us always,
until the end of time itself. Amen.

Interviews/testimonies

Hymns or songs

Chosen from:
A man there lived in Galilee (HON 3)
From the sun's rising (HON 150)
God forgave my sin (HON 167)
We have a gospel to proclaim (HON 532)

Intercessions

We pray to our Saviour Jesus,
enthroned on high as King of Kings,
saying, Lord of glory,
hear your people's prayer.

Jesus, King of Kings,
you are worthy to receive glory and power,
for you created all things.

Restore and heal your creation,
spoiled by human selfishness and greed.
May we show your love and care
in all our relationships,
with our world and with all people . . .
Lord of glory,
hear your people's prayer.

Jesus, Lord of Lords,
you are worthy to receive wisdom and might,
for by your blood you have purchased for God
people from every nation and race.
Restore and heal the nations of the world,
torn apart by hatred and violence.
May we demonstrate your righteousness
and justice . . .
Lord of glory,
hear your people's prayer.

Jesus, Sovereign over all,
you are worthy to receive honour and praise,
for you have made us a kingdom of priests
to serve our God.
Restore and heal your Church,
troubled and weakened by divisions
and disunity.
May we set aside our differences,
recognising that we are one in you . . .
Lord of glory,
**hear your people's prayer.
As we kneel before your throne
in praise and adoration,
we offer ourselves to you,
in the name of Christ our Lord. Amen.**

Our Father . . .

Hymn

Crown him with many crowns (HON 103) or
Christ triumphant (HON 81)

Final prayer

In our worship and witness
may we know God's presence.

With our families and friends
may we know God's love.

In our living and moving
may we know God's peace.

In our hearts and minds
**may we know God's blessing,
now and for evermore. Amen.**

PENTECOST

Pentecost always seems a particularly suitable time for ecumenical worship. Perhaps at Pentecost we are more aware that the Early Church was divided on the basis of location rather than denomination; perhaps church diaries tend not to be so full as at the other major festivals; or perhaps our awareness that the Spirit makes us one becomes more acute. Few will argue that the Church needs the fresh breeze of God's Spirit to disperse the staleness and blow away the sameness of its rituals and procedures, but it needs to be open for that to happen. When better than at Pentecost? Spontaneity and joy in worship are the keynote at Pentecost (though why restrict these to one Sunday a year?), but however much scope is given for open worship, some semblance of a framework is still necessary if the service is to involve several different traditions, not all of whom may feel comfortable with a less structured approach.

As with the less formal services for Easter and Ascension, considerable sensitivity and skill are required of those leading the act of worship: first, to ensure that Christians of all traditions feel included and able to worship God in that context; and second, to keep the proceedings under control so that no one individual or group can dominate or manipulate events for their own ends. The amount of freedom that can be given to *ad hoc* choice of hymns and songs will depend, as before, on the scope and flexibility of the musical resources, but however unspontaneous it may seem, do keep a few items up your sleeve that you know the musicians can play! If possible, try to order the songs and material to create times of quiet and reflection among the exuberance and anticipation, and break up the blocks of singing with readings and prayers. A clear time limit and end point are also helpful, so that those who need to leave may do so without feeling embarrassed.

Opening response

The Lord says, 'I will pour out my Spirit
on all people'.
**We live in him and he in us,
because he has given us his Spirit.**

When the Spirit of truth comes,
he will guide you into all truth.
**We live in him and he in us,
because he has given us his Spirit.**

We are all baptised by the one Spirit
into one body.
**We live in him and he in us,
because he has given us his Spirit.**

Opening hymn

Come down, O Love divine (HON 90) or
Father, Lord of all creation (HON 122)

Confession and absolution

Spirit of God,
we acknowledge your transforming power,
and confess our lack of faith.
Forgive and renew us;
fill us with your strength.

Spirit of God,
you came on the disciples as wind and flame,
giving them your power and authority.
We confess that our lives
show little of your power
and our witness little of your authority.
Forgive and renew us;
fill us with your power.

Spirit of God,
you come to bestow your gifts and blessings
on the Church.
We confess that we have been satisfied
with the earthbound poverty of our lives.
Forgive and renew us;
fill us with your life.

Spirit of God,
you come to equip your people
for witness and service.
We confess that we have resisted
your gentle yet insistent leading.
Forgive and renew us;
fill us with your love.

Spirit of God,
you come to make your people one
in the risen Lord.
We confess that we have maintained barriers
and tolerated division.
Forgive and renew us;
**fill us with your unity.
Release our lives from self-interest and guilt,
and our tongues to declare the praises
of Jesus Christ our Lord. Amen.**

Almighty God,
the Father of all mercies,
pardon and forgive all your sins
and by his Spirit make you one in him,
and with each other. Amen.

Songs

Two or three chosen from:
For I'm building a people of power (HON 135)
Gracious Spirit, Holy Ghost (HON 184)
Holy Spirit, we welcome you (Source 181)
I give you all the honour (HON 230)
I love your presence (Source 216)
Spirit of the living God (HON 454/455)
The King is among us (HON 483)

First reading

Romans 8:14-17 or
Acts 2:1-21

Songs

Two or three chosen from:
Bind us together, Lord (HON 60)
Filled with the Spirit's power (HON 131)
Jesus, restore to us again (Source 295)
Lord, we long for you (Source 337)
O breath of life (HON 356)
O thou who camest from above (HON 416)
Silent, surrendered (Source 456)

Second reading

1 Corinthians 12:3b-13 or
John 14:8-17

Time of open reflection

*As mentioned previously in the Easter service, the
value of this time, intended for sharing of insights
and prayer, depends very heavily on the leader*

enabling everyone present to share in it, rather than allowing one group or section to dominate the proceedings. If, as is likely, the tone of the service is basically joyful and exuberant, it would be wise to make this time quieter and more devotional, maybe incorporating some reflective songs and/or readings, provided time allows. As a response to a prayer or group of prayers, the song 'Alleluia' (HON 23) could be used, with words adapted to the context. The Lord's Prayer forms a suitable conclusion, joining together both the spoken and unspoken prayers offered previously.

Final hymn or song

Chosen from:
The Spirit lives to set us free (HON 494)
God's Spirit is in my heart (HON 180)
Angel voices, ever singing (HON 33)
Lord, the light of your love (HON 317)
Jesus is Lord (HON 270)

Final prayer

May God our heavenly Father
give us his Spirit of peace and unity.
Amen.

May Jesus Christ his Son
give us joy and confidence
as we walk by faith with him.
Amen.

May the Holy Spirit
make us one in worship, fellowship and mission
and guide us in the path of righteousness.
Amen.

HARVEST FESTIVAL

Those on the fringes of the Church often see Harvest Festival as one of the relatively few occasions during the year when they ought to turn up to a service. Regular churchgoers seem to regard it as second in importance only to Easter and Christmas – at least, if the amount of work they put into it is anything to go by! The origins of celebrating God's goodness to all people go back to Old Testament times, when three times each year the Israelites would offer him their thanks and praise for everything he provided. However, the form in which we now recognise Harvest Festivals dates only from the middle of the nineteenth century. This may have been a response to increasing industrialisation and a sense that society was starting to lose touch with the natural world, but, in an age when we have suddenly had to confront the damage which has been done to creation in the name of profit and progress, it has a particular relevance. Whatever differences they may have in matters of ritual and structure, Christians of all traditions are agreed that this is a priority issue, which they can address together. A clear indicator of this is the greatly increased popularity of liturgies in the Celtic tradition, which is particularly aware of God's creation and environmental issues.

For most churches Harvest Festival is a fairly movable feast, celebrated at some time between mid-September and mid-October (though Anglicans should note that it is not supposed to displace St Matthew or Michaelmas when these fall on a Sunday). From an ecumenical point of view this flexibility is an advantage, since the service can take place on the Sunday most convenient to all participating Churches. Coming as it does after the summer holidays, Harvest Festival is far enough away in time from the other major festivals not to be overshadowed by them, while its appeal is often to a rather wider constituency than just regular church attenders. The following service outline incorporates both thanksgiving for all that God has given us, and a recognition of our Christian responsibility to do what we can to act as good stewards of the world he has entrusted us with.

Opening response

To you, our Father in heaven,
creator of the smallest atom
and maker of the furthest galaxy,
we offer our sacrifice of praise.

To our Saviour Christ, his Son,
friend of the poorest beggar
and redeemer of the richest tycoon,
we offer our sacrifice of praise.

To the Holy Spirit of the Father and the Son,
enabler of the weakest Christian
and guide of the strongest character,
we offer our sacrifice of praise.

To God the three-in-one, present at creation,
present among us in Christ,
and present in our lives now,
we offer our sacrifice of praise.

Hymn

All creatures of our God and King (HON 9) or
Come, ye thankful people, come (HON 101)

Harvest thanksgiving

We thank God for all his good gifts to us:
for the vast expanse of the universe,
stretching far beyond our comprehension,
receive our thanks and praise.

For the tiniest insect and the mightiest beast,
exciting our amazement and delight,
receive our thanks and praise.

For the rhythm of the seasons
and the pattern of our days,
ordering our life and activity,
receive our thanks and praise.

For towering mountains
and unfathomable oceans,
filling us with awe and wonder,
receive our thanks and praise.

For bodies which work and play,
and minds which remember and imagine,
enabling us to share in the life of the world,
receive our thanks and praise.

For families to belong to
and friends to share with,
fulfilling our lives with companionship and love,
receive our thanks and praise.

For spirits created to worship you,
and hearts to respond to your love,
as we experience it in our Saviour Jesus Christ,
receive our thanks and praise,
as we rejoice in all you have made,
and in your promise to make all things new.
Amen.

Song

Dance and sing (HON 105) or
Shout for joy and sing (Source 450)

Confession and absolution

Our Lord God requires us to act justly,
love mercy, and humbly walk with him.
We confess that we have failed
to live up to our calling;
Lord, forgive and renew us.

For pursuing personal comforts
while turning a blind eye
to the destruction of your creation
in the name of profit and progress,
Lord, forgive us and renew our conscience.

For protecting our own interests
while closing our ears
to the cry of the helpless and vulnerable,
Lord, forgive us and renew our vision.

For stockpiling possessions and wealth
while ignoring the plight of the destitute
and disadvantaged,
Lord, forgive us and renew our compassion.

For concentrating on our own concerns
while holding at arm's length
your call to uphold justice and peace,
Lord, forgive us and renew our commitment.

For claiming allegiance to your kingdom
while failing to uphold its standards,
Lord, forgive us,
and renew our courage and zeal
to fulfil what you require of us,
as we follow the example
of our Saviour Christ. Amen.

Hymn

For the healing of the nations (HON 139)

Old Testament reading

Deuteronomy 26:1-11

Anthem

'The heavens are telling' (Haydn), *Favourite Anthem Book 1 and 3,* or 'For the beauty of the earth' (Cousins), *30 New Anthems for Mixed Voices*

New Testament reading

Luke 12:13-21 (or 30)

Hymn

For the fruits of his creation (HON 138) or
Inspired by love and anger (HON 252)

Address or meditation

Song

O give thanks (Source 384) or
Think of a world without any flowers
(HON 505)

Intercessions

Loving Father,
you care for the flowers that grow in fields,
and for the smallest creature.
How much more do you care
about the needs and sufferings
of the world you created.
As we bring before you our concerns
and prayers,
Father in heaven,
hear and answer us.

Land for cultivation
is overused or built on,
the landscape is disfigured,
those who work in it are in despair.
Give strength to those
who seek to live and work
in harmony with their environment,
and help us to be good stewards
of your creation.
Father in heaven,
hear and answer us.

Offices and factories are filled with stress,
unhealthy competition
sets colleagues against each other,
fear of unemployment
overshadows many at all levels.
Give courage to those who strive
to maintain the standards of God's kingdom
in their workplace,
and help us to act justly and honestly
in all our dealings.

Father in heaven,
hear and answer us.

Large organisations make financial decisions
with little care for others,
small businesses struggle to survive,
compassion is swamped
by a competitive spirit.
Give wisdom to those
who bear responsibility for major decisions,
and help us to put the interests of others
above our own.
Father in heaven,
hear and answer us.

Materialism dominates the thinking of society,
people stockpile money and possessions,
the gap between rich and poor
grows ever wider.
Give hope to those
who feel discouraged and helpless,
and help us not to give in to the temptation
to look after our own interests
but to give priority
to the needs of the poor and vulnerable.
Father in heaven,
**hear and answer us,
make us willing servants,
and help us to show your love and care,
for the sake of your Son,
Jesus Christ our Lord. Amen.**

Our Father . . .

Offering of gifts

Harvest is traditionally a time when we express our thanks to God for his goodness by helping to meet the needs of others. In the past this was done by collecting and distributing garden produce, with the more recent addition of non-perishable goods in cans and packets. Some Churches continue with this, particularly in more rural communities, but it causes certain problems, not least the practical issue of distribution, which has left many Church leaders wondering what to do with an excess of fruit and veg likely to demonstrate its perishable qualities in the short term. Even more vexed is the question of who should receive the gifts, and whether they either need or really want them, especially in more affluent areas. The rest of the world is also now much more familiar and accessible than ever before, and many Churches and ecumenical groups prefer to offer money or specific gifts to a particular cause, generally connected with the relief of poverty – quite a number of charities make a special Harvest appeal. It provides an excellent opportunity to emphasise Christian giving and make more of the offering and receiving of gifts. How this is organised will probably depend largely on the layout of the building and what is being collected, but it is usually very effective to invite everyone to come forward to present their gift. When this has been done, a corporate prayer can be spoken together:

Lord,
you have given us everything we have.
Our money, our possessions,
our lives are yours.
We can only give to you
what you have first given us.
Accept our offerings, and use them
to bring those who receive them
closer to your love,
in Jesus Christ our Lord. Amen.

Song

All that I am (HON 19)

Final prayer

In our waking and sleeping
Father, protect us.
In our working and resting
Jesus, encourage us.
In our coming and going
Spirit, direct us.
In our daily living and lifelong pilgrimage
God the Trinity
guard, guide and watch over us,
now and always. Amen.

Hymn

We plough the fields and scatter (HON 534) or
O Lord our God (Source 398)

ALL SAINTS' DAY

All Saints' Tide is traditionally one of the more important seasons of the Christian Year, lasting like Pentecost for eight days. Its significance in times past can be seen in the great number of Anglican churches dedicated to All Saints. Sadly the Christian celebration of the eve of All Saints' Day has become largely squeezed out by the secular festivities of Hallowe'en, with its masks, pumpkins and witches on broomsticks. While this has obvious pagan origins, it now functions mostly as a good excuse for a party, but Churches in many places have recently put on specifically Christian events to provide an alternative to this, and to the increasing interest in witchcraft and the occult. An act of worship on All Saints' Eve aimed at young families and teenagers might also divert some youngsters from the recent trend of 'trick or treat', which at times has become unpleasant and abusive.

However, while this may provide some motivation, the primary objective of worshipping God at All Saints' Tide is not to express opposition to the forces of evil (important though it may be to do so in other contexts). Rather, it provides the occasion for Christians to remind themselves of their hope of eternal life in Jesus Christ, and to give thanks for God's people who have gone before, in every age and place. Throughout our earthly pilgrimage we are inspired and challenged from time to time by a Christian friend or leader whose example has deepened our faith or changed the direction of our life. Those of us who are now more mature in faith might also bear in mind those who take their example from us, often without our realising it. This is an entirely positive message, which should be reflected in a thankful and joyful atmosphere for worship.

Although All Saints' Day itself falls on 1 November, the season lasts for eight days, so the Common Worship Lectionary and the Revised Common Lectionary recognise that many Churches will want to focus their celebration of it on the Sunday which falls in this period. Its distinctive themes are especially suitable for ecumenical worship. An alternative to Hallowe'en only makes sense on All

Saints' Eve, however, and this in particular has inspired some groups of local Churches to combine forces and organise not only an act of worship, but also a bonfire or firework party with suitable refreshments, something likely to be beyond the resources of a single congregation. The following service outline provides material which can be used in either context, but assumes that there will be some orientation towards families and children.

Opening praise response

Day and night the vaults of heaven
resound to the praise of God:
Holy, holy, holy is the Lord God Almighty.

All heaven falls down and worships you,
declaring:
**You are worthy, our Lord God,
to receive glory and honour and power.**

Saints and angels in heaven
stand around the throne singing your praise:
**To him who sits on the throne
and to the Lamb
be praise and honour, glory and power
for ever.**

Hymn

Holy, holy, holy is the Lord (HON 211)

Prayer of thanksgiving

For apostles and evangelists,
who taught the way of truth,
we give you thanks and praise.

For saints and martyrs,
who followed you without counting the cost,
we give you thanks and praise.

For leaders in the Early Church,
who strove to establish the truth,
we give you thanks and praise.

For monks, nuns and those whose devotion
shows us the path of prayer,
we give you thanks and praise.

For musicians, artists and poets,
whose skills beautify worship
and reveal your love,
we give you thanks and praise.

For teachers and pastors,
who by their faithful ministry
enable Christians to grow in faith and love,
we give you thanks and praise.

For evangelists and missionaries,
who by responding to the call of Christ
have brought others to know and love him,
we give you thanks and praise.

For all who by their example
have led us in the way of Christ
which leads to eternal life,
especially . . .
**we give you thanks and praise,
and seek your strength
to follow in their footsteps
until we join them in praising you
throughout eternity. Amen.**

Hymn

For all the saints (HON 134) or
Ye holy angels bright (HON 564)

Confession and absolution

**Our Father God in heaven,
we confess that we have failed
to live in the light of your love.
We have collected wealth and possessions,
instead of storing our treasure in heaven.
We have sought acclaim and status
in the eyes of others,
instead of pursuing the vision of your glory.
We have been distracted
by matters of little importance,
instead of upholding your kingdom.
Forgive our failings,
set our minds on things above
and fill our hearts with your everlasting love,
for the sake of Jesus Christ our Lord. Amen.**

Almighty God,
whose mercy endures for ever,
forgive all our sins,
pardon our earthbound ways,
and renew our fresh vision of heaven's glory,
where he lives and reigns for ever. Amen.

Hymn/song

All heaven declares (HON 14) or
City of God, how broad and far (HON 85)

First reading

Ephesians 1:11-23 or
Revelation 7:9-17

Song

As we are gathered (HON 40) or
Jesus, stand among us (HON 279)

Second reading

Matthew 5:1-12 or
Luke 6:20-31

Hymn/song

Let saints on earth in concert sing (HON 297)
or Moses, I know you're the man (HON 338)

Address

Response

*In an ecumenical setting, it is usually far more diffi-
cult to elicit a response from a congregation than in
a familiar local environment. One idea is the 'tree of
life', which is usually drawn on to several sheets of
paper attached to a large corkboard. Each worshipper has a piece of paper on which they can write the
name of a Christian who has influenced them in
their faith (or a specific occasion or event which
proved to be a 'defining moment'). These are then
pinned to the tree of life as an act of thanksgiving.
An alternative is to write the name of a Christian, or
church in another country, for whom the individual
has a particular concern, and pin it to the tree as a
symbolic prayer.*

Intercessions

We join with all of Christ's Church
throughout the world
in praying for its growth,
its unity and its witness, saying
Lord, you call us to be one;
help us to hear and respond.

We pray for the Church in places
where Christians are ill-treated . . .
Give courage to those who serve you
in the face of threats and violence,
and strengthen them in the knowledge
of your eternal presence and our prayers.
Lord, you call us to be one;
help us to hear and respond.

We pray for Christian leaders,
confronted with divisions,
discouragement and apathy . . .
Give patience to those
who feel their ministry has little effect,
and show us how to support and encourage
those you call to lead your people.
Lord, you call us to be one;
help us to hear and respond.

We pray for Christians who work for peace,
justice and reconciliation . . .
Give hope to those who struggle
against the world's prevailing ethos,
and help us to share their burdens and dreams.
Lord, you call us to be one;
help us to hear and respond.

We pray for Christians
who share the good news of Jesus Christ
with those who do not yet know you,
especially among the underprivileged . . .
Give joy to those engaged in mission,
and enable us to be effective witnesses
to your saving love.
Lord, you call us to be one;
help us to hear and respond.

We pray for ourselves,
that in our lives and fellowship
we may demonstrate our unity in Christ . . .
Give us vision to see
beyond present divisions and barriers
to a time when your people will be one,
and the earth be filled with the glory of God,
as the waters cover the sea.
Lord, you call us to be one;
help us to hear and respond,
with actions born of faith,
faith born of love,
and love flowing from hearts
filled with your Spirit,
through Jesus Christ our Lord. Amen.

Our Father . . .

Hymn/song

Brother, sister, let me serve you (HON 73) or
May the grace of Christ our Saviour
(HON 333)

Final prayer

God our Father,
guard us on our journey
through this earthly life.
**May we travel with the hope of heaven
in our hearts.**

Christ our Saviour,
forgive us when we leave the narrow way,
and redirect our feet on to the right path.
**May we travel with the joy of heaven
in our hearts.**

Holy Spirit of God,
guide us when the way is unclear
and keep our eyes fixed
on the prize to which we are called.
**May we travel with the vision of heaven
in our hearts.**

Father, Son and Holy Spirit, blessed Trinity,
bring us in your good time
to the place you have prepared for us,
to sing and praise you with the saints for ever.
**May we travel knowing you are before us,
beside us and within us,
through your Son, Jesus Christ our Lord.
Amen.**

Hymn/song

Thy hand, O God, has guided (HON 518) or
From the sun's rising (HON 150)

Blessing

OTHER OCCASIONS

The Church has always arranged its worship around an annual pattern of events, based on seasons and festivals. While this is still followed to some extent by many Churches and Christian traditions, the increasing complexity of the world means that there is now a greater awareness of other occasions on which a liturgical response is particularly appropriate. Many of these will be 'one-off' events, but some will recur on a regular basis. They do not always sit very comfortably in the context of the Christian year, but provide an ideal opportunity for Christians to join together across the denominational divides for worship and service. The following selection of services are designed for the most frequently used occasions, but they can be adapted easily enough to other circumstances where necessary. If at times the occasion can seem rather secular, it is nonetheless a great opportunity for a congregation to reach out to parts of the community with which it would otherwise have little contact, and the quality of the worship may well determine what contact is possible in the future. A service for Remembrance is included in this section because of its connection with the civic and wider communities.

WEEK OF PRAYER FOR CHRISTIAN UNITY

The Week of Prayer for Christian Unity occurs annually from 18 to 25 January, and both nationally and locally is the most significant ecumenical event of the year. Although it happens during the Epiphany season, it is now regarded almost as a season in its own right, and apart from the liturgical and prayer materials made available on a national basis, many local Churches Together groups make it one of the highlights of their year. The primary focus is inevitably Christian and Church unity, but the week finishes very appropriately on the feast of the Conversion of St Paul, emphasising Christ's commission to bring the Gospel to all people. Whatever else Christians may disagree about, there can be little argument over that!

It would be easy to forget that for the first 1500 years of the Church's existence there were no denominations as we now recognise them, though the early Christians had plenty of disagreements and divisions to contend with. By the same token we should recognise that, while we properly condemn division and disunity, some denominations were formed because of the frustration of a genuine desire to bring about necessary change in the Church. Martin Luther and John Wesley are just two examples of Christians whose spiritual journey resulted in the formation of a new church structure. Sadly, however, this has not always been the case, and the history of the Church, especially in this century, is littered with instances of new Churches and Christian groups forming for no reason other than minor disagreements not being resolved. The Week of Prayer for Christian Unity has to recognise this past, together with its continuing effects in the present, while at the same time underlining that this need not shape the future. And rather than trying to impose an artificial uniformity on the various traditions, the Week of Prayer for Christian Unity seeks instead to draw out the underlying unity between Christians of all traditions.

The following outline service assumes that Christians from a variety of traditions and backgrounds will be coming together in worship on the Sunday of the Week of Prayer for Christian Unity, and that shared mission and evangelism may be a key focus in that. The Peace is included near the end of the service as a mark of unity and reconciliation. The material is equally suitable for ecumenical events at any time of the year.

Song
As we are gathered (HON 40) or
Jesus, stand among us (HON 279)

Opening praise response
God, who is rich in mercy,
has made us alive in Christ;
though we were dead in our sins,
we have been saved by grace.

Once we were without hope
and without God in the world;
**Now we have been brought near to him
through the blood of Christ.**

Christ is our peace,
for he has pulled down the dividing wall
of hostility;
**through him we all have access to the Father
by one Spirit.**

In him the whole building is joined together
to become a holy temple in the Lord.
**In him we are being built together
to become a place where God lives by his
Spirit.**

Hymn

Filled with the Spirit's power (HON 131) or
Love divine, all loves excelling (HON 321)

Thanksgiving

Gracious Father,
we look back at all you have done
for your people down the ages
and offer you our thanks.
Lord of all,
accept our praise.

For giving us your Son,
by whose death we are made one,
Lord of all,
accept our praise.

For leading us from the slavery of sin
to freedom in Christ,
Lord of all,
accept our praise.

For calling us to be your people
and filling us with your Spirit,
Lord of all,
accept our praise.

For guiding us on our pilgrimage of faith
towards our common goal,
Lord of all,
accept our praise.

For promising to be with even two or three
who meet in your name,
and for your presence with us now,
Lord of all,
**accept our praise,
and make us one in worship and fellowship,
through Christ our Lord. Amen.**

Song

For I'm building a people of power
(HON 135) or
May the grace of Christ our Saviour
(HON 333)

Confession and absolution

**Lord of the Church,
we confess to you
the sins which have divided your people:
we have built walls of fear and distrust;
we have created barriers
of prejudice and suspicion;
we have broken the unity
for which Christ died.
We are sorry, and ask you to forgive us.
Replace our pride and selfishness
with your peace and joy,
and restore us to fellowship
with you and one another,
for your holy name's sake. Amen.**

Almighty God,
whose mercy is on all who turn to him,
have mercy on us,
pardon and deliver us from all our sins,
and make us one with each other and him,
through Jesus Christ our Lord. Amen.

Song

A new commandment (HON 4)

First reading

1 Corinthians 1:10-17 or
Ephesians 4:1-16

Anthem

'How lovely are thy dwellings fair' (Brahms),
Anthems Old and New

Second reading

John 17:20-26

Sermon

Song

We believe in God the Father (HON 530) or
From many grains (HON 149)

Intercessions

We bring to God
our prayers for the Churches represented here,
for our common worship and mission,
and for the ecumenical process
which draws us together in closer relationship.
Lord, receive our prayer,
and make us one in your love.

We commit to you all the Christian Churches
meeting here in your name,
and those congregations
who as yet feel unable to join them.
May we grow closer to each other
in our one faith and one Lord,
recognising the points
where as yet we are not of one mind,
but building on those
where we find common ground . . .
Lord, receive our prayer,
and make us one in your love.

We commit to you
those activities which we undertake together:
shared worship, mutual fellowship
and united mission.
May we pull down barriers of division,
learn to respect different insights,
and seek ways to overcome the issues
which still separate us . . .
Lord, receive our prayer,
and make us one in your love.

We commit to you
our efforts and discussions
for bringing together Christians
of different traditions,
especially in this community.
May we not be deterred
by inflexible structures
or discouraged by slow progress,
but strive to build up our unity in the Spirit
through the bond of peace . . .

Lord, receive our prayer,
**and make us one in your love;
unite us in heart and mind,
and give us the vision
of your eternal kingdom,
through Christ our Lord. Amen.**

Our Father . . .

*An unusual and effective way of symbolising our
unity in Christ is to use a portable electric paper
shredder, of the sort that might be found in a church
office (or failing that, borrow someone else's!).
Invite the congregation, or if numbers are too high,
one or two representatives of the participating
Churches, to write on a sheet of A4 paper some
aspect of our past disunity or present division
which needs to be destroyed – suitable examples
might be suspicion, judgementalism or refusal to
listen to each other, though other more specific ones
may spring to mind. These are then fed into the
shredder and symbolically destroyed, before moving
on to the Act of Commitment.*

Act of Commitment

People of God,
will you honour your common faith,
learn from your varied insights
and work for the common good?
We will, with the Lord's help.

People of God,
will you come together
in worship and fellowship,
combining the riches of your traditions
and sharing your journey of faith?
We will, with the Lord's help.

People of God,
will you work together
to bring the Gospel of Christ
to this community,
bearing witness to his love for all people
and showing his compassion
to the needy and unloved?
We will, with the Lord's help.

God grant us the vision,
the courage and the strength
to go forth in his name
and uphold his kingdom,
rejoicing in our one faith and one Lord.

Song

Bind us together (HON 60)

The Peace

As God's people,
bear with one another, forgive one another
and let love bind you together in true unity.
Let the peace of Christ rule in your hearts.
The peace of the Lord be with you.
And also with you.

Song

Father, Lord of all creation (HON 122) or
From the sun's rising (HON 150) or
Rejoice! (Source 438)

Final prayer

Father,
guide us
as we journey together on the road to heaven.
Open our eyes to see your truth.

Jesus,
be alongside and travel with us
as we journey together on the road to heaven.
Open our hearts to receive your love.

Spirit,
dwell within us and encourage us
as we journey together on the road to heaven.
**Open our lives to share your love
with others. Amen.**

Blessing

CHRISTIAN AID WEEK

Most Churches probably regard Christian Aid Week as something of an organisational obstacle course. Not that anyone would dispute its immense value, either in terms of raising funds for the world's neediest people, or as a means of highlighting these needs to those who might not be so aware of the problems. In order to combine resources where possible, in many areas collecting is now organised ecumenically, and a shared act of worship makes very good sense as a way of launching this, and encouraging those who will be spending the next few days knocking on doors. This need not be particularly formal, though it might be helpful to find a speaker with expert knowledge in this area. Those who receive Christian Aid mailings will know that they usually produce liturgical resource material based on the particular theme and projects for the year. The following outline for a Christian Aid Week service is in no way intended to usurp the very good material that Christian Aid produces each year. Rather it can be used to supplement that, or be adapted for specific local circumstances. The material could just as easily be used at other times of year if a group of local Churches is supporting a particular project to help the poor and deprived, whether at home or abroad.

Opening prayer

O Lord our God,
may you be praised throughout eternity
as our loving Father.
To you belong all greatness and power,
glory and majesty and splendour,
for everything in heaven and on earth
is yours.
Your kingdom lasts for ever;
it will never fade or fall.
You rule the whole universe and all that is in it;
wealth and honour,
power and authority come from you alone.
We thank and praise you,
for everything we have
comes from your goodness.
As we offer our gifts of time and energy,
ability and money,
we give you now what you have given us,
for everything finds its source in you,
the one true and living God,
whom we come now to worship. Amen.

Hymn

Eternal Ruler of the ceaseless round
(HON 115)

Opening Psalm

In the council of heaven
God stands and gives his judgement, saying,
**'How long will you judge unjustly
and show favour to those who do wrong?**

'Give justice to those who are weak,
and have no one to protect them;
Uphold the rights of the vulnerable and poor.

'Rescue the poor and needy;
Deliver them from the grasp of the evildoer.'

Rise up, O God,
and according to your mercy judge the earth,
for all the nations belong to you alone.

Hymn

Cry 'Freedom!' (HON 104)

Confession and absolution

We acknowledge before our heavenly Father
our selfishness and lack of care for the wellbeing of our fellow human beings, saying
Lord, in your mercy,
hear us and forgive us.

We have accumulated possessions and wealth
without thinking of those
who have no resources;
Lord in your mercy,
hear us and forgive us.

We have rejoiced in our own comforts
while ignoring the plight
of the poor and needy;
Lord, in your mercy,
hear us and forgive us.

We have looked after our own welfare
while turning a blind eye to poverty and evil;
Lord, in your mercy,
hear us and forgive us.

We have prided ourselves on personal morals
while failing to work for justice and peace;
Lord, in your mercy,
hear us and forgive us.

We have heard the good news of Jesus
without passing it on to the hopeless
and despairing;
Lord, in your mercy,
**hear us and forgive us,
and strengthen us to work
for the good of all people. Amen.**

Almighty God,
who pardons all who turn to him
in sincere repentance,
have mercy on you,
forgive all your sins,
and make you what he would have you be,
through his Son, Jesus Christ our Lord. Amen.

Hymn

Forgive our sins as we forgive (HON 141)

First reading

Amos 5:11-15, 21-25 or
Micah 6:6-8

Second reading

Luke 18:18-30 or
James 2:1-10

Hymn

Heaven shall not wait (HON 207) or
Inspired by love and anger (HON 252)

Reflection

Song

Jesus Christ is waiting (HON 268)

Intercessions

We commit this world to God,
in all its beauty and joy,
and its desperate need and sadness, praying:
Lord, as we bring you this prayer,
we offer ourselves to your service.

We think of those
whose suffering stems from natural causes:
flood or drought, storm or heat,
earthquake or famine . . .

May the world be united
in bringing relief and aid to the needy,
and may our generosity of spirit
reflect to them the love and care of God.
Lord, as we bring you this prayer,
we offer ourselves to your service.

We think of those
whose suffering results from conflict and hatred:
victims of civil war, torture
and racial prejudice . . .
May all people and races
be united in condemning inhumanity,
and may we demonstrate
the equality of all before God.
Lord, as we bring you this prayer,
we offer ourselves to your service.

We think of those
whose suffering is caused by neglect
and rejection:
victims of abuse and exploitation,
bigotry and discrimination,
violence and cruelty . . .
May our society always protect
the weak and vulnerable,
and may we show compassion
to those left on the margins.
Lord, as we bring you this prayer,
we offer ourselves to your service.

We think of those
whose suffering is forgotten by everyone else:
the lonely and bereaved,
the elderly and handicapped,
the depressed and despairing . . .
May their needs and pain
be recognised by the caring agencies,
and may we display to them
Christ's love for the unloved and disregarded.
Lord, as we bring you this prayer,
**we offer ourselves to your service
and commit ourselves to your kingdom,
to bring love, joy and peace
to the world we live in,
for the sake of Jesus Christ our Lord. Amen.**

Act of Commissioning

If at all possible invite all the collectors and officials to stand at the front of the church. If space or num-bers preclude this, they should stand in the places where they have been seated. The laying on of hands could be included, but is unlikely to be practical, and in any case is usually reserved for much longer-term acts of public ministry.

Minister: As you go from house to house, calling on friends and neighbours, will you take with you the love of Christ for all humankind?
Collectors: In the Lord's name, we will.

Minister: As your friends collect the offerings of love and concern, will you support them and pray for them?
Others: In the Lord's name, we will.

Minister: As you take with you the good news of Christ's love, will you too be generous in your gifts for those in great need in . . . ?
All: In the Lord's name, we will.

Minister:
Lord, we ask you to bless your servants
now about to offer their time and energy
to collect money for relief and aid.
May they know you with them
in delivering envelopes
and calling to collect them,
that those who give
may also be touched by your presence,
and those who benefit from the gifts
may see in the generosity of others
your compassion for all who are in need. Amen.

Hymn

O Lord, all the world (HON 378) or
Will you come and follow me? (HON 560)

Final prayer

**Father, send us out
with eyes which can see the need around us.
Christ, send us out
with hearts full of your love and compassion.
Spirit, send us out
with lives dedicated to being good news
for the poor and needy.
And the grace of our Lord Jesus Christ . . .**

REMEMBRANCE

Few services are more loaded with expectations and preconceptions than those that take place on Remembrance Sunday. While everyone is aware of more recent conflicts and the devastation caused by them, the generation with direct memories of the Second World War is inevitably declining. If that group have memories and emotions to address on Remembrance Sunday, younger people are likely to have a more pacifist agenda, so that most of those who take part in a Remembrance service will attend with an individual package of feelings and opinions.

Nonetheless, Remembrance Sunday is still marked in almost every community across the country, sometimes on an ecumenical basis. It is a good occasion for Churches to participate in worship across denominational boundaries – the experiences and thoughts which underlie it are common to all traditions, and there is no set liturgical format. In addition, the Remembrance service is often regarded as a civic event, at which uniformed organisations and representatives of the local community may be present on a formal basis, whether or not they regularly attend church.

Whatever tradition they are based on, Remembrance services tend to be fairly formal and structured, both out of deference to those with painful memories, and to enable people from a range of backgrounds to participate meaningfully. The following outline is loosely based on Morning Prayer, and incorporates both the usual two minutes' silence and prayers which reflect the concerns of the wider community. While the material has been written with this particularly in mind, however, it would also be suitable for any occasion when Christians join together from all traditions to pray for peace and remember the victims of conflict. The formality and sombreness of the atmosphere could make any less traditional elements jar slightly, though there are a number of fine poems which would not feel out of place (for example those by Wilfred Owen). It might also be helpful to arrange for portable display boards to be covered with images of war and its consequences and prominently positioned so that after the service the congregation can quietly reflect and pray if they wish to.

Opening response

Glorify the Lord with me;
let us exalt his name together.
Those who look to him are radiant;
their faces are never covered with shame.
Taste and see how good the Lord is;
blessed are those who take refuge in him.
Turn from evil and do good;
seek peace and pursue it.

Hymn

O God, our help in ages past (HON 366)

Prayer of approach

Almighty God,
we come before you,
the Creator and sustainer of all that lives,
whose love knows no ending.
We offer thanks and praise
for our deliverance from conflict and danger;
we remember with gratitude the courage
of those who laid down their lives in war
that we might live in peace and freedom;
we commit to your care all who suffer
through the violence and degradation of war;
we acknowledge before you
our sins and failings
and those of society,
confessing them openly
and seeking your pardon:

Confession and absolution

We repent of the pride and arrogance
that creates divisions
rather than heal suffering.
Lord, have mercy;
forgive us and help us.

We repent of the fear
that has made us run away from conflict
rather than seek reconciliation.
Lord, have mercy;
forgive us and help us.

We repent of the apathy
that has made us turn away
from pain and injustice
rather than pursue righteousness and peace.
Lord, have mercy;
forgive us and help us.

We repent of the selfishness
that has ignored the plight
of the poor and vulnerable
rather than share the compassion of Christ.
Lord, have mercy;
**forgive us and help us to be peacemakers
for the sake of the kingdom of your Son,
Jesus Christ our Lord. Amen.**

The God of all mercy
forgive all your sin and wrongdoing,
fill your hearts with his love and peace,
and make you one
in the service of his kingdom,
through Christ our Lord. Amen.

Hymn

We will lay our burden down (HON 538)

First reading

Isaiah 2:1-5 or
Ezekiel 37:1-14

Second reading

John 15:9-17 or
Hebrews 11:1-16 or
Hebrews 11:17-28, 39-40

Hymn

For the healing of the nations (HON 139) or
Inspired by love and anger (HON 252)

Sermon

Act of Remembrance

We stand before God holding in our memories all those who have lost their lives in the blood-shed and carnage of war. Some we remember because we knew and loved them; some we remember because they are mourned by others; some we honour though they have no loved ones to remember them. We give thanks for those whose death has enabled others to live, celebrating their courage and steadfastness.

A centrally placed candle is lit, or members of the congregation come forward in silence to light a votive candle in memory of the fallen. Two minutes silence follows.

They shall not grow old,
as we who are left grow old.
Age shall not weary them,
nor the years condemn.
At the going down of the sun,
and in the morning,
we will remember them.
We will remember them.

Hymn

Peace is flowing like a river (HON 412) or
Through the night of doubt and sorrow
(HON 517)

Intercessions

We bring to God in our prayers
those who suffer
through being caught up in conflict and war:
For members of the armed services,
whose training and tasks bring daily risks;
Lord, hear our prayer.

For senior officers and political leaders,
whose decision-making
bears heavy responsibility;
Lord, hear our prayer.

For those injured and disabled
in conflict or service,
whose infirmity continues;
Lord, hear our prayer.

For those traumatised by their experiences,
whose faith and hope have been shattered;
Lord, hear our prayer.

For innocent victims of bullet and bomb,
whose lives and homes have been destroyed;
Lord, hear our prayer.

For those who have paid the ultimate price
and lost their lives as a result of war,
whose families and loved ones grieve for them
silently and alone,
Lord, hear our prayer,
which we offer in the name of Jesus Christ
the Prince of Peace, Amen.

Alternative response
Kyrie (HON 290)

Act of thanksgiving

For courage and hope in times of trouble,
we thank you, Lord.
For the example and challenge of those
who have laid down their lives for others,
we thank you, Lord.
For the peace and freedom we now enjoy,
we thank you, Lord.
For those who serve their country
to provide protection and security
for their fellow-citizens,
we thank you, Lord.
For strength to face present conflict and danger,
and for the hope of eternal life
in our Saviour Jesus Christ,
we thank you, Lord. Amen.

Hymn

All people that on earth do dwell (HON 17) or
Lord, for the years (HON 310)

Final prayer

Committing ourselves to the cause of peace
and justice, we pray to our heavenly Father:
Lord, make us channels of your peace.
Where there is hatred,
may we bring love.
Where there is hurt,
may we bring healing.
Where there is doubt,
may we bring faith.
Where there is despair,
may we bring hope.
Where there is darkness,
may we bring light.
Where there is sadness,
may we bring joy.

As we forgive, may we be forgiven;
as we give, so may we receive.
Lord, make us channels of your peace.

Blessing

EVANGELISTIC SERVICES

Your reaction to the idea of an evangelistic service will probably depend on your perception of what might happen on such an occasion. For some, even the thought of evangelism will bring back unpleasant memories, fear of overt emotionalism, and the possibility of manipulative tricks being used to force a 'decision'. Others will react very positively, perhaps having come to faith themselves as a result of such an event, or seen new life come into their church. Having read this far you may have concluded already that this isn't 'your scene', but before you write the whole idea off, it would be as well to remember that in many larger towns and cities, as well as a good number of smaller ones, the concept of an ecumenical evangelistic mission is already well established. This isn't a particularly modern development. In the eighteenth century the Wesleys concentrated their efforts on places where large numbers of ordinary folk lived, while a hundred years later Moody and Sankey were also renowned for preaching to large congregations. In this century Billy Graham has been perhaps the best known large-scale evangelist, and while he himself has appeared primarily in London, live relays have enabled his events to be screened in communities across the country, in events organised by groups of local Churches. The late David Watson was one of the best known in an honoured line of Anglican evangelists, but his city-wide missions were largely ecumenical, even if one or two Churches took prime responsibility. On a practical level, few single Churches are well enough resourced to tackle such a large-scale project, but if all are agreed on the basic message, there is every reason theologically why such missions should be ecumenically organised.

Admittedly there are certain issues to deal with, the thorniest usually being which local Church a new convert should be introduced to. While these are not within the scope of this book, it is vital that they are addressed, and procedures agreed on, long before any launch service, praise evening or final celebration is planned. It should also be remembered that while Churches of a more evangelical tradition may show particular enthusiasm for this kind of venture, others of a different hue may be equally committed to mission and want to be included. A true ecumenical spirit embraces Christians of all traditions, and seeks to include those who may see faith from a slightly different perspective, rather than exclude any who might possibly pose a threat to a particular approach. Any ecumenical evangelistic liturgy has to encompass the range of views within the participating Churches.

Finally there is the obvious but often forgotten reality that evangelism is aimed primarily at reaching out to those who aren't regular church attenders, and are therefore likely to be unfamiliar with worship and liturgy. There isn't much point in inviting non-churchgoers to a special church event if, when they arrive, they find themselves unable to relate to what's going on. Feeling excluded and out of one's depth are guaranteed to deter even the most sympathetic of souls, while being hectored, judged or patronised generally have the same effect. An effective liturgy for evangelism will therefore be user-friendly in its language and concepts without 'dumbing down', and will be careful not to invite people to make responses for which they don't yet feel ready.

The following outline is based on common practice, and assumes that at least some of those present will be exploring concepts of faith with which they are not fully familiar. But most people would expect confession and intercession, and a couple of simple responses are also included. Unavoidably, the highlights will include an address or presentation explaining the Christian faith, and possibly a dramatic sketch or mime which underlines this message. At least some of the hymns should be well known to those outside the regular membership of the Church (though they don't all have to be traditional), and have words with which they can identify.

Opening prayer

Lord,
we are mere dots on the face of the earth,
infinitely small in the vast expanse
of the universe.
From the tiniest atom to the furthest star,
everything exists because of you.
In your greatness and majesty
you reign over all,
nothing happens
outside the scope of your kingship.
And yet despite our smallness,
our preoccupation
with trivial personal interests,
your love for us is beyond measure.
So we turn towards you,
perhaps uncertain of the consequences,
but seeking to discover more of your love,
of your reality, and of eternity.
Open our eyes to see more of your glory,
our minds to know more of your truth
and our hearts to experience
more of your love,
as we see it in Jesus Christ. Amen.

Hymn

Make way, make way (HON 329) or
Praise, my soul, the King of heaven
(HON 422)

Opening response

Lord,
you are far beyond our limited understanding;
we cannot find our own way to you.
**Thank you for making yourself known to us
in Jesus Christ.**

Lord,
you are in heaven,
far away from the pressures and pains
of our earthly existence.
**Thank you for coming to share our life here,
our joys and sorrows,
in Jesus Christ.**

Lord,
you are far above our fallible nature;
we cannot earn our place with you.
**Thank you for bringing us back to you
through Jesus Christ.**

Lord,
you are far greater and more loving
than we could ever imagine.
**Thank you for extending your love to us,
undeserving as we are.**

Song

Lord Jesus Christ (HON 311) or
The King of love my shepherd is (HON 484)

Confession and absolution

We have said words we immediately regret;
we have acted in ways we are ashamed of;
we have harboured thoughts
we know are unworthy
Not daring to look to you, we say,
Lord, have mercy on us.

We have failed to keep our promises;
we have acted carelessly
and without regard for others;
we have condoned what we know to be wrong.
Not daring to look to you, we say,
Lord, have mercy on us.

We have turned away when faced with need;
we have promoted our own concerns
above the welfare of others;
we have behaved as though you played no
part in our lives.
Not daring to look to you, we say,
Lord have mercy on us.

We have failed even to live
up to our own standards,
and often feel oppressed by guilt;
we cannot come into your presence
with clean hands and hearts.
Not daring to look to you, we say,
**Lord, have mercy on us;
forgive all our sin;
take away our guilt and shame;
and set us free to praise your name,
through Jesus Christ our Lord. Amen.**

God, who hears us when we cry to him
from the depths of our despair,
have mercy on us,
pardon all our sins and failings,
and bring us the joy of eternal life
in his Son, Jesus Christ our Lord. Amen.

Song

I am trusting thee, Lord Jesus (HON 223) or
I'm accepted (HON 239)

First reading

Acts 9:1-19a or
Acts 17:22-31 or
1 John 4:7-16

Second reading

Mark 2:1-12 or
Luke 15:11-32 or
Luke 19:1-10

Drama/Presentation

Hymn

Just as I am (HON 287) or
It's me, O Lord (HON 256)

Address

Prayer

Listening to the voice of Jesus, we answer:
Lord, as we hear your call,
help us to respond.

You invite us to come
exactly as we are, into your presence,
knowing we are accepted and forgiven.
Lord, as we hear your call,
help us to respond.

You invite us to lay our burdens on you
and find rest deep within.
Lord, as we hear your call,
help us to respond.

You invite us to leave the past behind
and follow you.
Lord, as we hear your call,
help us to respond.

You invite us to seek your righteousness
above all,
so that everything else falls into place.
Lord, as we hear your call,
help us to respond.

You invite us to share your ministry
of compassion to the poor and needy.
Lord, as we hear your call,
help us to respond.

You invite us to take up our cross
and follow you.
Lord, as we hear your call,
**help us to respond
by loving and serving you,
our Saviour and friend. Amen.**

Hymn

I, the Lord of sea and sky (HON 235) or
Will you come and follow me (HON 560)

Final prayer

Lord God,
faith is being sure of what we hope for,
and certain of what we cannot see.
We ask you to give us the gift of faith,
to put our trust in you,
to receive your forgiveness and love,
and to follow in your footsteps
until we reach the home in heaven
you have promised us,
through Jesus Christ our Lord. Amen.

Blessing

HEALING SERVICES

Thirty or forty years ago the concept of a healing service was almost unheard of. The charismatic renewal was only just beginning to impact on the mainstream denominations. The Church has always offered intercessions for the sick and suffering as a normal part of regular worship, but the thought of a whole liturgy centred around praying for healing, accompanied by the laying on of hands, would have been at best

unfamiliar to most Churches, or worse, viewed with considerable hostility as a threat to good order. It was mostly the preserve of independent groups such as the Guild of St Raphael. Now the situation has almost been reversed. Healing services are normal and accepted in all the main traditions, and where they do not take place this is more likely to be caused by a lack of resources than by antipathy. Churches in a more Catholic tradition often prefer to link healing with the eucharist, which certainly makes sense spiritually and theologically, though it can bring problems in an ecumenical context.

Where there are fears about healing services they usually revolve around two areas – the 'cringe factor' and the fear of disappointed expectations. Unfortunately these fears are not entirely groundless, and too many people have had unhappy experiences. Excessively emotional behaviour sits uneasily in a public act of worship, and while God has given us the capacity to release emotional pressures in different ways, this should never cause embarrassment or offence to others. In an ecumenical setting this is especially important, since Churches will react in quite different ways to such phenomena. Making false claims about the prayers for healing, or building up expectations which are then dashed, has left some disillusioned about everything to do with Church, and whoever is responsible for leading worship must be very clear about the realities of the situation. At the same time, many have found healing services to be of great personal and spiritual benefit, sometimes much to their surprise – awareness of the pitfalls is no reason for avoiding the Christian healing ministry, since it follows the example and commands of Christ, and has been practised since the earliest days of the Church.

Much has been written about healing services, and at greater length than is possible here, but the following three questions need to be considered:

1. How formal or informal should the worship be?
Greater formality has the advantage of a firmer structure, which usually acts as a brake on over-the-top emotionalism, but the potential disadvantage of feeling rather staid and starchy. Greater informality generally leads to

a sense of freedom and warmth, enabling everyone to feel relaxed, but great care needs to be taken that the healing ministry does not become trivialised, and that individual responses do not get out of hand. The ideal is to achieve a good balance between the two, but this may be affected by the building or worship area where the service is taking place, the inclinations of those leading it, and the expectations of those present.

2. How should the ministry of prayer with laying on of hands be organised?

There are several ways to approach this, and your final decision will probably depend on specific local factors. In a eucharistic context it is often best to administer the laying on of hands at the communion rail, after the sacrament has been received, but this is unlikely in an ecumenical setting. The communion rail is a good place in any event, visible to the rest of the congregation but without them being able to hear what is said. However, it may be preferable to use a side-chapel or similar space. Ideally, two ministers (lay or ordained) should ask God's blessing on each one who comes to them, but in a smaller building there may be room only for two or at most three ministry points. These should be situated where conversation cannot easily be overheard by anyone else. It is also essential to establish and maintain clear time limits on this process, which is intended as a way of bringing people into the healing presence of Jesus through prayer. While some of those who seek prayer may understandably need extended counselling, an act of worship is not the place for this – such help should be given later, privately, away from the gaze of others, or else the rest of the congregation may become restive about when the service will actually end. The aim of this is not to restrict the work of the Holy Spirit in any way, but simply to enable everyone present to experience the presence and healing love of God without distraction. The use of oil for anointing the sick is increasing in many of the mainstream Churches, and for some will be an important element. Others may react with caution, however, and sensitivity will be necessary in discussing beforehand whether this should happen.

3. Who should be involved?

Some Churches have a team of people who have been trained to exercise this kind of Christian healing ministry, others operate on a more *ad hoc* basis. In an ecumenical healing service it is important to involve members of as many participating congregations as possible, lay as well as ordained. At the same time, those who exercise this ministry should have received some suitable instruction beforehand, and should be widely respected individuals – denominational allegiance takes a lower priority than personal qualities such as sensitivity and integrity. Initially at least, it is probably wise to ask the local ministers to suggest suitable candidates to share in the praying and laying on of hands, and give their blessing to those invited. There should be a clear understanding that little more than a brief prayer will be required during the service itself, though arrangements may need to be made to deal with those whose need of help will be over the longer term. Bear in mind, too, that healing services are liable to attract some people whose personal needs lead them into attention-seeking and demanding behaviour. While they deserve the same consideration and care as anyone else, they may look for more than this, with the potential for causing offence and embarrassment to others. Should this start to happen, it generally indicates that some other kind of help is required. The person concerned should be taken to one side discreetly and sensitively, so that others can also receive ministry through prayer without being distracted.

The following service outline is based on a non-eucharistic healing service for Pentecost, but it could be used just as well at other times of year, with the addition if necessary of suitable seasonal material.

Opening response

If anyone is in trouble
they should pray to God.
If anyone is rejoicing
they should sing praises to God.
If anyone is sick
they should seek God for healing through prayer.

The prayer offered in faith
brings wholeness to the one who is ill;
it is God who will raise him up.

Hymn

How sweet the name of Jesus sounds
(HON 220) or
O for a thousand tongues to sing (HON 362)

Responsorial Psalm

Your love, O Lord, reaches to the heavens,
your faithfulness to the skies;
continue your love to those who know you.

Your righteousness is like
the towering mountains,
your justice like the unfathomable deep;
continue your love to those who know you.

We feast on the abundance of your house,
and drink from the river of your delights;
continue your love to those who know you.

With you is the fountain of life,
and in your light we see light;
continue your love to those who know you,
and your righteousness
to the upright in heart.

First reading

Acts 2:1-11 or
Acts 3:1-16 or
1 Corinthians 12:1-11

Song

Peter and John went to pray (HON 416) or
Peace, perfect peace (HON 414)

Second reading

Matthew 8:5-13 or
Luke 10:1-12 or
John 5:1-15

Sermon/Meditation

Song

Be still and know (HON 52) or
Give thanks with a grateful heart (HON 154)

Intercessions

Waiting for the coming of power from on high,
we pray:
Lord, bless and heal us;
fill us with your Spirit.

Holy Spirit,
fill us with your power
and strengthen us to serve you better.
Make us bold in word and action
to proclaim your saving and healing love . . .
Lord, bless and heal us;
fill us with your power.

Holy Spirit,
fill us with your wisdom
and help us discern your purposes.
Make us see more clearly how you call us
to live for you day by day . . .
Lord, bless and heal us;
fill us with your wisdom.

Holy Spirit,
fill us with your gifts
and equip us to work more faithfully for you.
Help us recognise the ministries
to which you call us . . .
Lord, bless us and heal us,
fill us with your gifts.

Holy Spirit,
fill us with your peace
and increase our confidence in your love
in every situation.
Help us share that peace and love
with everyone in need of them . . .
Lord, bless and heal us;
fill us with your peace.

Holy Spirit,
fill us with your love
and show us those in distress
to whom we can bring your compassion.
Make us open to you
and able to show your love in action . . .
Lord, bless and heal us;
fill us with your love,
and make us one in heart and mind
to serve you for the glory of Jesus Christ
our Lord. Amen.

Song

Be still, for the presence of the Lord (HON 53)
or
Lord, we come to ask your healing (HON 319)

Confession and absolution

Almighty God,
we confess that we have sinned against you
in our thoughts, our words, our actions.
We have grieved your Holy Spirit
and resisted his healing work in us.
We are sorry,
and repent of all our wrongdoing.
Forgive us, we pray, heal our hurts
and fill us with the fire of your love,
that we may live to the praise and glory
of Jesus Christ, your Son, our Lord. Amen.

Almighty God,
who freely gives his Spirit
to all who turn to him,
grant you forgiveness for all your sins,
peace in your hearts
and power to live for him day by day,
through Jesus Christ our Lord. Amen.

Time of Prayer with Laying on of Hands

By definition this part of a healing service needs a degree of flexibility and a capacity to respond to needs that arise. However, thought should also be given to those who are not receiving or have already received prayer for healing. Peaceful music, whether recorded or performed live by a choir or music group, provides a more helpful background for personal meditation than silence, and it may be preferable to ask those taking part to restrict their words to a formula for blessing, recognising that some will want to expand on their concerns at a later stage. The following are formulae that may be found helpful:

May you be filled in body, mind and spirit,
with the healing power of the Holy Spirit of
Jesus.

May you know the healing love of Christ
in every part of your life
through the power of his Holy Spirit.

May the love of the Father,
the grace of the Lord Jesus,
and the peace of the Holy Spirit
fill your heart and mind now and for ever.

May God's healing power fill your life
and make you whole,
as you respond to the love of Christ
through his Holy Spirit working within you.

If it is decided to anoint those receiving prayer with the oil of healing, this should be preceded by a simple formula such as:

I anoint you with this oil for healing
in the name of the Father, the Son,
and the Holy Spirit . . .

Final prayer

Holy Spirit of Jesus,
you came on the disciples in the upper room
in the form of wind and flame,
making them bold to proclaim the good news
and heal the sick.
Fill us with that divine energy,
and make us channels of your healing love,
to bear witness to your truth
and display your love to those in need.
through Jesus Christ our Lord. Amen.

Hymn

Immortal love, for ever full (HON 243) or
We will lay our burden down (HON 538)

Final response and blessing

Love of the Father
watch over us.
Love of the Son
enfold us.
Love of the Spirit
uphold us.
Love of the Trinity
heal us and make us whole.

CIVIC SERVICES

There are many reasons why a local community might want to gather for worship. It may be to mark a significant event, to remember a notable occasion, to celebrate an achievement or anniversary, to honour or commemorate an individual or organisation, or even to pray for the community and those who serve it. Traditionally the main parish church of the town would have been a prime venue for such services, or maybe in some places a large nonconformist church, but there is an increasing trend for them to be organised ecumenically. This makes good sense both as a fairer representation of the community and as a statement that the Christian faith is far greater than any one tradition.

Civic services of any sort have a number of conditions imposed on them, either by the focal point of the event or by the make-up of the congregation. The liturgy will almost certainly have to embrace in some way the person, organisation or event at the centre of the celebration. This may not be too difficult when Christian virtues such as care and compassion are in the forefront, but requires rather more creativity when dealing with secular organisations, such as sports clubs, business concerns or the retail trade – my personal favourite was an annual carol service for guide dogs and their owners! There is also the likelihood that quite a few people may be present who do not often attend church, and are unfamiliar with words and rituals regular churchgoers take for granted. A certain formality or traditionalism may also be expected or assumed. But if this kind of civic service makes one or two different demands, these are far outweighed by the opportunity it presents to establish the Church at the heart of the community and for Christians to be reminded that their faith is never lived in isolation from the rest of the world.

It would be impossible to outline a liturgy to cover every civic eventuality. Some will be joyful and celebratory occasions, others more sombre and thoughtful; some will centre on an organisation or institution, others on an individual's life; some will look back to the past, others will commit the future to God. The following simply offers a few suggestions of a general nature which will cover a variety of scenarios. They will probably need some adaptation, and please note that although the intercessions contain ten different biddings, no more than four or five should be selected for use on any one occasion – otherwise 'drooping eyelid syndrome' will set in among the congregation!

Opening responses

Sing to the Lord a new song;
sing to the Lord, all the earth.
Sing to the Lord, praise his name;
proclaim his salvation day by day.
Declare his glory among the nations,
his wonderful acts among all people.
Great is the Lord, and most worthy of praise;
he is to be worshipped above all other gods.

Hymn

Praise to the Lord, the Almighty (HON 427) or
Sing to God new songs of worship (HON 447)

Opening prayer

God our Father,
Creator of the universe,
sustainer of all life, sovereign over all people,
we sing and declare your praise.
Your faithfulness provides all our needs;
your hand guides and protects us
on our journey;
your strength renews our confidence
and energy.
Your mercy is everlasting,
your love never fails.

Lord Jesus Christ,
born as one of us, friend of sinners,
Saviour of the world,
we celebrate and rejoice in your love.
Your example inspires us;
your death saves us;
your risen life fills us with hope
for our journey.
Your mercy is everlasting,
your love never fails.

Holy Spirit of God,
eternal presence of the Father and the Son,

Comforter, Enabler,
we serve the Kingdom in your strength.
Your gifts equip us;
your peace governs us;
your presence never leaves us on our journey.
Your mercy is everlasting,
your love endures for ever.

Hymn

Jubilate, everybody (HON 284) or
Let us with a gladsome mind (HON 302)

Confession and absolution

We acknowledge in God's presence the sins
we have committed and the good we have
failed to do, saying:
Merciful Lord,
grant us your pardon and peace.

We have revelled in the good things of this life,
but ignored the needs in the world around us.
Merciful Lord,
grant us your pardon and peace.

We have looked after our own interests,
but silently condoned oppression and injustice.
Merciful Lord,
grant us your pardon and peace.

We have steered away from conflict,
but avoided the pain of peacemaking
and reconciliation.
Merciful Lord,
grant us your pardon and peace.

We have spoken fine words,
but forgotten to translate them into action
for your kingdom.
Merciful Lord,
grant us your pardon and peace.

We have kept up an appearance of religion,
but failed to give it any substance in our daily
lives.
Merciful Lord,
grant us your pardon and peace,
and strength to live each day
in the light of your love,
through Jesus Christ our Lord. Amen.

Hymn

Judge eternal, throned in splendour
(HON 285) or
Restore, O Lord (HON 434)

First reading

Leviticus 18:9-18 or
1 Chronicles 29:10-20 or
Nehemiah 5:1-12

Psalm

Praise the Lord, O my soul;
I will sing praise to God as long as I live.
Blessed is the one whose help is in God,
whose hope is in the Lord.
He is the maker of heaven and earth,
the sea and every living thing;
he will remain faithful for ever.
He upholds the cause of the oppressed,
and provides food for the hungry.
He sets prisoners free,
and restores sight to the blind;
he lifts up those who are bowed down,
and loves those who do right.
The Lord watches over the alienated
and sustains the vulnerable;
he thwarts those whose ways are wicked.
The Lord reigns for ever,
over all ages and peoples;
praise the Lord, O my soul.
(adapted from Psalm 146)

Second reading

Matthew 22:15-22 or
1 Timothy 2:1-7 or
James 2:14-26

Sermon/Address

Hymn

Heaven shall not wait (HON 207) or
Jesus Christ is waiting (HON 268)

Intercessions

(select as appropriate)

Lord our God,
you have taught us to pray for those in authority,
whose decisions influence the lives
of many people.

We come to you now with our prayers
for the nation, the community
and those who play a vital role within them.
Lord, hear us as we pray,
bless and guide them.

We pray for places of education
and those who work or study in them:
schools, colleges and universities;
headteachers and principals;
teaching and non-teaching staff;
pupils and students,
especially those in this community . . .
In their teaching and learning
may they grow in knowledge of you.
Lord, hear us as we pray,
bless and guide them.

We pray for hospitals,
surgeries and care homes,
and those engaged in the work
of caring and healing:
doctors, nurses, carers and counsellors,
particularly those to whom
we entrust our health . . .
In their caring may they bring
your healing love to the suffering.
Lord, hear us as we pray,
bless and guide them.

We pray for those responsible
for law and order:
judges and lawyers;
police and law enforcement officers;
prison and probation officers;
politicians and lawmakers,
whose work enables us to live in security . . .
In their undertaking
may they hold to your standards of justice.
Lord, hear us as we pray,
bless and guide them.

We pray for directors and managers
of businesses large and small,
and those whom they employ:
in banks and finance houses;
industrial concerns and craft workshops;
information technology and service providers,
remembering also the unemployed . . .
In their daily tasks
may they act with integrity and honesty.

Lord, hear us as we pray,
bless and guide them.

We pray for those on whom we rely
for personal safety and convenience:
workers in public transport,
road haulage and distribution;
the emergency services and rescue teams;
the armed forces and defence agencies . . .
In their actions may they recognise
the responsibility they bear.
Lord, hear us as we pray,
bless and guide them.

We pray for those
who give their time and energy
on a voluntary basis:
in schools and children's groups;
among young people and families;
among the vulnerable and elderly . . .
In their willing service
may they find their reward in you.
Lord, hear us as we pray,
bless and guide them.

We pray for those who guide and direct
the affairs of our local community:
the mayor and local councillors;
staff in the town hall and other departments
which meet our everyday needs;
social and community workers . . .
In their duties to the public may they realise
that they are answerable first to you.
Lord, hear us as we pray,
bless and guide them.

We pray for those who govern our national life
and influence society by their decisions:
politicians in government and opposition;
administrators and civil servants;
broadcasters, journalists,
and all who work in the media . . .
In their discharge of leadership
may they acknowledge you
as the source of all authority.
Lord, hear us as we pray,
bless and guide them.

We pray for ourselves,
asking for wisdom to know
what we should do in your name;

courage to stand firm
against corruption and evil;
strength to continue serving you by faith;
and hope to hold before us
until that day when we shall answer to you
for the lives we have led.
Lord, hear us as we pray,
**bless and guide us
in our working and resting,
our coming and going,
that in all we do we may honour you
and live for your glory. Amen.**

Our Father . . .

Hymn

God is working his purpose out (HON 172) or
Lord, for the years (HON 310)

Final prayer

Father God,
keep our eyes fixed on our calling in you;
make us faithful and true.

Christ our Lord,
keep our hearts filled with your love
and compassion;
make us loving and open;

Spirit of God,
keep our lives free from sin
and dedicated to your glory;
make us pure and holy;

Holy God, blessed Trinity,
keep us abiding in you;
now and for evermore. Amen.

Blessing

A NEW YEAR/ NEW START SERVICE

The following service example was the ecumenical celebration put together at St Francis of Assisi and Ruxley Methodist Church for the start of the new millennium. The ideas were generated at an open invitation brainstorming evening and put together by the clergy team, with a great deal of help from others. Some material came from the CCBI *NewStart Worship Resource Book 2*, the rest was written especially for the day. The intention was to devise a liturgy which would be very user-friendly for non-churchgoers, so the language was deliberately accessible and the hymns well known. The role of Zacchaeus being interviewed was played by a member of the congregation wearing a smart suit, generally agreed to be much more effective at depicting the character than the usual dressing gown and tea-towel look! The questions asked are included as an example of how such an 'interview' might be directed, though we focused specifically on Zacchaeus leaving behind his old life and making a new start with Jesus. Abraham was also considered in a similar vein, but time considerations precluded this. An excellent hymn if you prefer to use Abraham as the example is 'One more step along the world I go' (HON 405). The shredder proved to be a versatile visual aid and symbol (see the service outline for the Week of Prayer for Christian Unity) and despite initial misgivings about it being a bit gimmicky, the sight of our balloons soaring into a remarkably blue January sky, carrying our hopes and dreams for the future, was very moving and inspiring. This is too expensive and complex to organise other than for a very big event, and if done more than occasionally would lose its impact, but it is nonetheless worth considering for those special events which are specifically forward looking. Please also note that despite some comments in the media most commercially available release balloons are bio-degradable, and if you are in the vicinity of a major airport you should let their air traffic control know, as the balloons may show up on their radar screens.

Opening praise

I said to the man who stood at the gate of the year: 'Give me a light, that I might tread safely into the unknown.' And he replied: 'Go out into the darkness and put your hand into the hand of God. That shall be to you better than light and safer than a known way.' So I went forth, and finding the hand of God, trod gladly into the night. And he led me towards the hills and the breaking of a new day.

Song
Lord of all hopefulness (HON 313)

Responsive Psalm

This world belongs to God, and everything in it;
**The whole earth is his,
and everything that lives on it.**

He formed dry land to stand between the oceans;
The rivers flow through it to fill the sea.

Who is worthy to ascend the hill
of God's holy place?]
**Those whose actions are honest,
whose motives are honourable,
whose thoughts and words are trustworthy.**

These people will receive God's blessing;
the God who saves them
will honour and uphold them.
**Their heart's desire is to see God;
They long to see the face of Jacob's God.**

You mighty gates, steeped in victory,
open wide your portals to the King of Glory!
Let the King of Glory enter in majesty.

Who is the King of Glory?
**The Lord who is mighty and powerful
to defeat the forces of evil.**

You mighty gates, steeped in victory,
open wide your portals to the King of Glory!
**Let the King of Glory enter
in might and power.**

Who is the King of Glory?
**The Lord of all heaven and earth,
he is the King of Glory.**

Song
Make way (HON 329)

Praise response

Lord of all time:
who was, and is, and will be for ever,
we praise and worship you.

Silence

Lord of all space:
present in all places, here with us now,
we praise and worship you.

Silence

Lord of all life:
power of love, strength to change,
Spirit within.
We praise and worship you.

Silence

Our Father . . .
If preferred, this could be sung to the tune 'Auld lang syne'. The music is available in Hopes and Dreams.

Bible reading
Luke 19:1-10

Interview

The questions below give an idea of how to structure the interview, in this case with Zacchaeus.

1. Tell us a bit about yourself, Zacchaeus – your job, your hobbies, friends, favourite meal, places you've been to . . .
2. Did you enjoy your work as a tax-collector?
3. What did your friends think? Did they approve of you collecting taxes for the Romans?
4. Didn't you have a really fantastic life-style?
5. How did you come to meet Jesus? Was it an ambition of yours?
6. What was it about him that interested you?
7. But why on earth climb a tree to see him – were you trying to hide?
8. What did Jesus say to you?
9. Since you met him your life's been completely turned round. What are the big differences and how have your friends reacted?
10. So what are you going to do with your life from now on?
11. What would you say to anyone else who wanted to follow Jesus?

Song

Seek ye first the kingdom of God (HON 442)

Shredding

See page 77, under Week of Prayer for Christian Unity. At this point in the service, before the confession, selected members of the congregation were invited to write on a sheet of A4 paper those things that they wanted to leave behind in the old millennium, before making a new start. The picture of the paper being shredded is a powerful reminder that God does not remember our sins and failings.

Confession

Lord Jesus,
sometimes we do not want to admit
that we have done wrong;
we refuse to face up to what needs changing
in our lives.
We are sorry for not obeying you.
Please forgive us and help us.

Lord Jesus,
sometimes we think we can live without you;
we act as though you did not matter.
We are sorry for not letting you rule our lives.
Please forgive us and help us.

Lord Jesus,
sometimes we are reluctant
to move on from where we are now
because we feel comfortable,
we worry about what might happen.
We are sorry for not trusting you.
Please forgive us and help us.

Absolution

God, who is full of mercy and love,
forgive all our sins,
take away our guilt and fear,
and fill us with the hope and joy
of his Holy Spirit,
through Jesus Christ our Lord. Amen.

Carol

It came upon a midnight clear (HON 253)

Prayers for renewal

Eternal God,
our history and our hopes are held

in the wounded hands of your risen Son.
As we look into time unknown,
we pray for the people and the tasks
that will weave the pattern of our future days.

To people we have yet to love,
and answers we have yet to find:
Loving God,
guide us and lead us.

Through challenges we have yet to face
and to courage we have yet to need:
Loving God,
guide us and lead us.

Through suffering we have yet to feel
and pain we have yet to know;
Loving God,
guide us and lead us.

In the renewing of our nation
and in the inspiring of new life:
Loving God,
guide us and lead us.

Towards dreams we have yet to follow
and horizons we have yet to see:
Loving God,
guide us and lead us.

In the freedom of hope
and the promise of all creation:
Loving God,
guide us and lead us.

God of love,
you call us to follow paths as yet unknown.
Teach us not to be afraid, and give us your grace,
that we may be drawn together
in life and love and peace,
and in trusting, find our future life in you,
through Jesus Christ our Saviour.
Amen.

From *Worship Resources for the Millennium*, Vol. 2
Copyright © NewStart 2000 Ltd.

Song

The Spirit lives to set us free (HON 494)

Thanksgiving

For the worship and witness of God's Church
over the last two thousand years:
we thank you, Lord.

For the commitment of Christian people
down the centuries
who have left their mark on the world:
we thank you, Lord.

For the presence of your Spirit with us
day by day,
comforting, challenging and guiding us:
we thank you, Lord.

As we start out on this third millennium
since the birth of Christ:
we ask you to help us.

As we seek a new start
for the poorest people in the world:
we ask you to inspire us.

As we look for new ways
to share your good news
with our own community:
we ask you to guide us.

As we build our hopes and dreams
into the reality of your kingdom:
we ask you to strengthen us.

From *Worship Resources for the Millennium,* Vol. 2
Copyright © NewStart 2000 Ltd.

Writing cards

Just before the end of the service, every member of the congregation was given a tie-on label on which to write their own hopes and dreams for the new millennium. After the final song, the congregation tied these to balloons before going out into the glorious winter sunshine and releasing them simultaneously.

Song
Lord, for the years (HON 310)

Blessing

Song
You shall go out with joy (HON 571)